X

PRAISE FOR *When You Say Yes But Mean No*

"Silencing conflict is a universal problem in companies of all shapes and sizes. Yet people fail to recognize when they are caught in this dangerous syndrome until it wreaks havoc on their relationships. Leslie Perlow's excellent book teaches you how to detect early symptoms and avoid detrimental situations. For your own career success and for the success of your company you should start putting her lucid and practical ideas to work today."

—ADRIAN J. SLYWOTZKY, coauthor of *The Profit Zone*

"*When You Say Yes But Mean No* is an invaluable resource for anyone working in an organization. People have a tremendous amount of knowledge and insight about what it takes to be successful. The challenge, though, is creating the kind of environment in which they feel comfortable speaking up and dealing directly and genuinely with peers, subordinates, and superiors. Leslie Perlow's book contains critical insights and practical suggestions about how to create more open and honest relationships. If you put her ideas to work the net result is sure to be a healthier and more productive organization.

—RAYMOND GILMARTIN,
chief executive officer, Merck & Co., Inc.

"This is a remarkable book that once started I had to read from cover to cover. The 'don't rock the boat' syndrome is one of the silent killers of the modern corporation. It is a real breakthrough to learn how conflict brought out into the open can be a creative and sustainable force for the benefit of any company and its decision makers. Everyone knows how unspoken dissent is lurking below the surface but few business leaders have the confidence to deal with it. Leslie Perlow shows how it can be done in a well researched and readable style."

—ALAN PARKER, president, Whitbread Hotel Company

"*When You Say Yes But Mean No* compellingly demonstrates the devastating and inescapable consequences of keeping silent and not engaging in difficult conversations about doubts, concerns, and differing points of view. It should be required reading for executives everywhere and the first book assigned to new business school students."

—BRUCE PATTON, Harvard Negotiation Project, coauthor of *Getting to YES* and *Difficult Conversations: How to Discuss What Matters Most*

Also by Leslie A. Perlow

Finding Time: How Corporations, Individuals, and
Families Can Benefit from New Work Practices

When You Say Yes But Mean No

HOW SILENCING CONFLICT
WRECKS RELATIONSHIPS AND
COMPANIES... AND WHAT YOU
CAN DO ABOUT IT

LESLIE A. PERLOW

CROWN
BUSINESS
NEW YORK

A NOTE FROM THE AUTHOR

In due respect to everyone who graciously shared their experiences
with me, I have changed their names to protect their identities.
I have, however, used real company names wherever possible.
I am greatly indebted to everyone with whom I spoke.
While their names do not appear in print, they know who they are—
and the book could not exist without their incredible generosity.

Copyright © 2003 by Leslie A. Perlow
All rights reserved. No part of this book may be
reproduced or transmitted in any form or by any means,
electronic or mechanical, including photocopying, recording,
or by any information storage and retrieval system, without
permission in writing from the publisher.

Published by Crown Business, New York, New York.
Member of the Crown Publishing Group, a division of Random House, Inc.
www.randomhouse.com

CROWN BUSINESS is a trademark and the Rising Sun colophon
is a registered trademark of Random House, Inc.

Printed in the United States of America

Design by Robert C. Olsson

Library of Congress Cataloging-in-Publication Data
Perlow, Leslie A., 1967–
When you say yes but mean no: how silencing conflict wrecks relationships
and companies... and what you can do about it / Leslie Perlow.—1st ed.
1. Conflict management. 2. Management. I. Title.
HD42 .P47 2003
658.4'053—dc21   2002151029
ISBN 1-4000-4600-9
10 9 8 7 6 5 4 3 2 1

First Edition

to Joy

CONTENTS

*When You Say Yes
But Mean No*

INTRODUCTION

Covering Up Rather Than Confronting Difference

THE MEMBERS of Versity's top management team seemed of one mind and ready to tackle the challenges facing their business. After a long day of team-building exercises and animated discussions about the company's future, they remained in their seats around a horseshoe-shaped table in a nondescript hotel conference room in Redwood City, California. Nine hours earlier, Peter, the company's soft-spoken chief executive officer, alluding to the crisis that the company faced about its strategy, had stated: "Our goal today is to all end up on the same page. We are currently moving in an unclear direction, and we need to be more clear."

Two months earlier, Peter had joined Versity and had hired a team of professional managers to help the four young founders to continue to expand their company. Now Jill, the self-assured head of public relations, having volunteered to lead the day's events, handed each of them a hotdog-shaped balloon, the kind that clowns give out at the circus. She asked them to take turns expressing their reactions to the day's events, including whether their expectations had been met and how they felt at the moment. After people spoke, they were to attach their balloon to the previous speakers' balloons, thus gradually creating a sculpture. Hal, the newly hired acting head of marketing, went first. "My expectations were met," he said. "Jill, you did a great job. We made some great progress today. . . . It feels great. I am excited . . . passionate . . . committed to the future." Dave, the newly hired head of product development, continued: "The consistency of vision and purpose is good to hear. We are pretty similar in what we are thinking. We are not automatons, but consistency is good." Jim, the new chief financial officer, boasted: "I am happy. I thought today was going to be a lot uglier. I expected battles. Yet things were remarkably consistent." Peter added: "It was a good starting point. Jill did a good job keeping us moving. I enjoyed today." The company's founders also expressed relief at the consistency they had heard. Clyde, the business brains behind the company, sounded pleased: "After today I am more comfortable that we are all on the same page." And Howie, the technical guru, shared: "It was neat to have everyone in the same room together. I was quiet because I wanted to hear what others had to say. I wanted to hear from the new people, with new ideas and new perspectives. It seems we all pretty much agree on what is going on. Thank you."

Peter ended the day's events by suggesting that everyone go downstairs to the hotel bar and have a beer to celebrate. The meeting broke up, but before heading to the bar and then out for dinner, most people gathered to admire their balloon sculpture, with its bright colors and all its contortions, twists, and turns.

Everyone had gone into the day's events deeply worried about a lack of consensus. They were particularly concerned that a schism was developing between the founders and the new professional managers over the company's purpose. Yet, at the end of the meeting, they all expressed joy about their level of agreement.

Privately, though, many despaired. When the four founders gathered the next night to reflect on the "vision meeting," as they called it, Howie snickered, "What a waste. Nothing was accomplished." He paused, took a deep breath, and continued, "We are directionless. We used to know what was going on. But we lost our goal. Now we have no focus. We are bobbing in water. We have no momentum. We should be reacting and changing, yet nothing is happening." The other three nodded in agreement.

The professional managers also had outwardly expressed pleasure about the consensus everyone voiced. However, they too felt that nothing had been accomplished. They weren't as surprised by this result, though, since they had been through this kind of meeting many times before. While Peter didn't mention it to anyone on his management team, he was convinced they would need to meet again to reach closure on their goals.

After the meeting the professional managers continued to question whether the core market for their educational product should remain college students or should instead become professors. Indeed, no attempt had been made to answer this fundamental question at the meeting. And deep down, they all knew they still disagreed. No one, however, dared raise the issue. The founders continued to focus on college students, the company's target market since its start. The professional managers, including Peter, shifted their focus toward professors—the market they had come to believe had to be the company's future focus. No one said anything about the divide. They all just forged ahead, pursuing the goal they perceived to matter most. The company, however, sorely lacked the human and financial resources to pursue these two paths simultaneously.

Still, no one wanted to confront this reality and force a choice. Rather, they wanted to preserve their relationships and their business. Both Peter and his new hires, as well as the company's four founders, deeply appreciated how much they needed one another to make the company a success. They also recognized that speed was of the essence and that they had no time to waste. Not wanting to put their relationships or their business in jeopardy, no one spoke up. Within nine months, the company was bankrupt.[1]

Whether between colleagues, friends, or family members, the tendency to cover over differences rather than confront them is all too common.[2] In important relationships—from the boardroom to the bedroom—we often find ourselves smiling and nodding when deep down we couldn't disagree more. We believe that the best thing to do to preserve our relationships and to ensure that our work gets done as expeditiously as possible is to remain quiet. What we are doing is silencing conflict.[3]

SILENCING CONFLICT

Conflict is not by nature good or bad. Conflict simply means difference—difference of opinion or interests.[4] Throughout this book, I use the words *conflict* and *difference* interchangeably. And I use the term *silencing conflict* to refer to anytime people do not fully confront their differences. Often people speak openly about their differences but do so in the hallway, or around the water cooler, or behind closed doors—out of earshot of the person with whom they differ. Sometimes people do mention their differences to one another but fail to do so in a way that they are understood.

Silencing conflict encompasses a range of behaviors, from never speaking differences aloud to ending a discussion of differences before they are fully understood. We are silencing conflict if we become quiet despite perceiving that the other party does not understand why we think, feel, or believe as we do. We are also silencing conflict if we end a discussion before we've done our best to understand the "why" behind the other party's thoughts, feelings, or behavior.[5]

THE COSTS OF SILENCE

We often associate conflict with its negative forms—petty bickering, a bloody fight, physical violence, even war.[6] But conflict can also be a source of creative energy; when handled constructively by both parties, differences can lead to a healthy and fruitful collaboration, a co-creation or co-construction of new knowledge or solutions.[7] With constructive conflict, the end result is different from and better than any of the initial, individual perspectives; opposing parties come together to realize their respective goals and work together toward a win-win outcome.[8] When we silence conflict, we avoid the possibility of negative conflict, but we also miss the potential for constructive conflict.

When differences are kept quiet, we limit creativity, learning, and effective decision making. Creativity and learning require novel ideas—seeing and doing things in new ways—but when differences are considered unacceptable, novel ideas are less likely to emerge. When we don't feel comfortable expressing our differences, we are also less likely to disclose errors and take risks, both of which are necessary for learning to occur. And when we do not share perspectives and information, decision making can suffer, because we are less apt to explore the pros and cons of various solutions.

Silencing conflict also affects individual performance. When we feel we can't share our differences, we may lose interest in and disengage from our work. The result can be increased stress, lack of motivation, high job turnover, and sometimes even sabotage.[9]

Even worse, although we often silence conflict because we believe it is the right thing to do, the best thing to do, the only way to preserve important relationships and get on with the task at hand, acting on this belief may create the consequences we most dread.[10] Silencing conflict about important issues with peo-

5

ple for whom we care deeply can result in disrespect for, and devaluing of, those same people. It can create a whole underworld in which differences become an increasingly destructive force.[11] Each time we silence conflict, we create an environment in which we're all the more likely to silence next time. Silencing conflict creates resentment, anger, and frustration in a person. These negative emotions turn into a powerful and harmful agent, making one feel increasingly self-protective in the relationship and therefore all the more fearful about speaking up. As a result, more acts of silence follow. We get caught spinning in a vicious "silent spiral," making the relationship progressively less safe, less satisfying, and less productive.[12]

In addition, when there is pressure to go fast, people are all the more likely to silence their differences to keep things moving as quickly as possible. And, the act of silencing, in turn, creates negative consequences that often result in problems that take time and attention to resolve. With the mounting work from these additional problems, the sense of urgency intensifies, and so too does the pressure to silence. Ultimately, the pressure to go fast feeds on itself, further intensifying the destructive nature of the silent spiral.

Had the management team at Versity—both the founders and the new professional hires—recognized the costs of silence and instead spoken up about their differences at the offsite vision meeting, the future of their company might have been different. Instead of pursuing two independent paths, the team might have found a shared purpose that built on their different perspectives and goals. But all this potential was lost when the members failed to discuss their differences.

THE STORY BEHIND THE STORY

For me this book began its life one January afternoon in 1999, when Clyde stopped by my office at the University of Michigan.

Clyde had been one of 160 undergraduate business majors in my organizational behavior class the previous year. Now, he explained, he needed one course to remain an active student during the semester. Would I supervise an independent study for him? He told me he was planning to spend the semester working with three other students who had founded an online education company called Versity.com, short for "university." I agreed to oversee Clyde's independent study, and before the conversation was over, I asked if I could see the company for myself.

I'm an organizational ethnographer. This means that, like an anthropologist, I spend large amounts of time in the field observing a culture—the only difference being that the field is the office and the culture is the corporate environment. My previous ethnographies had covered a range of workplaces, from major American corporations to European and Asian businesses.

However, when, a week later, I drove to Versity's office in Ypsilanti, a blue-collar suburb on the outskirts of Ann Arbor, I had no intention of embarking on another research project. I visited only because I wanted to meet these young entrepreneurs and see a dot-com in action. Many were already making millions of dollars in Silicon Valley, but in my college town of Ann Arbor, Michigan, dot-coms were still a novelty.

During my first visit, I was impressed by the dedication, maturity, and accomplishments of the four young founders. After that initial visit, I found myself returning on several more occasions. Each time, I intended to stop by for only a few hours, but I ended up staying late into the night, filling notebook after notebook with observations. A couple of visits eventually turned into a nineteen-month obsession.

One of the surprises from my early visits was that the organizational dynamics inside this dot-com were not so different from those in the larger, more traditional, bricks-and-mortar businesses I'd previously studied. The big difference was the speed and intensity of the office. Everything happened at an accelerated pace—from business development to product release—and everything seemed to have higher stakes. These factors, I quickly realized, brought otherwise hidden issues into sharp relief, revealing aspects of work relationships that are often difficult to discern in the typical one- to two-year study of an ethnography. Thus, Versity provided a way for me to gain insight into the fundamentals of my field—organizational behavior—by giving me a richer understanding of how people interact, and with what consequences. It was the equivalent of an epidemiologist studying a disease during a major epidemic. The conditions were optimal to observe patterns or trends that might otherwise be latent.

Studying Versity further provided an opportunity to explore how speed itself affects our interaction patterns and ultimately our relationships and our work output. In a society in which the goal so often is to find ways to do more in less time, studying Versity provided a rare opportunity to glimpse where we may well be headed. I have always been a student of time, trying to understand how we use time at work, why we use it in the ways that we do, and what consequences our patterns of time usage have for ourselves, our co-workers, and the organizations in which we work. Studying Versity enabled me to further explore what happens when our interactions suddenly increase in pace.

By the time I completed the fieldwork, I'd taken approximately ten thousand pages of notes and had conducted hundreds of interviews with everyone involved with the company. I had observed everything from top-level management meetings to hallway gossip to late-night beers at local bars. During the months I spent at Versity, I observed people's actions and listened to their public conversations, but I also developed relationships that made people comfortable in sharing private thoughts and feelings with me.[13] I therefore had the privilege of listening to people speak to each other, *and* of knowing what they were *not* saying. I noticed early on that colleagues weren't being completely frank with one another. They didn't want to endanger the success of their venture, so they shied away from differences. They smiled when they were seething; they nodded when deep down they couldn't have disagreed more. They pretended to accept differences for the sake of preserving their relationships and their business. And, the more people silenced themselves, the more pressure they felt to silence themselves again next time.

Observing the tendency to silence conflict at Versity stirred my curiosity about the existence of such a phenomenon in other domains. How much of what I had observed was simply due to the pervasive sense of urgency in the dot-com world? I conducted interviews with a range of different people to explore that question. I interviewed friends, family members, students, and strangers. I was not looking for a random sample. I was just seeking to better understand where silencing conflict might occur and at what cost. I spoke to doctors, lawyers, investment bankers, and consultants. I spoke to officers in the military and directors of nonprofits. I spoke to those who ran companies and to those who reported to them. I spoke to people just out of college and to others ready to retire. I talked to people about their work lives and about their home lives.

When I began telling people about the idea behind this book—namely, the silencing of conflict and its unacknowledged costs—they would invariably respond, "That's the story of my company," or, "You are writing about my marriage." One of my business school students, who had previously been an investment banker, told me, "You could be writing my biography."

In the four years since Clyde came to my office to ask for course credit, I have learned about the destructive effects of silencing conflict, on everything from business partnerships to personal relationships. I have seen how these acts of silencing build on each other, creating the dangerous syndrome I call the "silent spiral." And I have come to appreciate how the need for speed fuels the silent spiral. But I have learned as well that we can free ourselves from this syndrome. And more than that, if we can effectively express our differences, we can instead create a constructive spiral of speaking up.

In order to share the stories I've heard and the lessons I've learned, I have divided the book into three parts. Part I uses "episodes," or single snapshots, of silencing conflict to elaborate the concept—to show where it occurs, how it gets perpetuated, and at what costs. The story of the rise and fall of Versity, detailed in Part II, illustrates how episodes of silencing build on each other to create the silent spiral, inflicting cumulative damage on relationships and performance at work. The story of Versity further shows how the need for speed makes the silent spiral all the more vicious. Part III then focuses on the pressing need to express our differences—and how to do so most effectively. At the end of the book, I return to the Versity story to explore one final question: What might have been the outcome had the members of Versity effectively expressed their differences?

PART ONE

The Unacknowledged Costs of Silencing Conflict

CHAPTER ONE

The Many Forms of Silence

E AGER TO protect important relationships and to ensure that our work gets done as efficiently as possible, we often silence conflict on core issues. We believe that this is the best way to preserve our ability to work together. Yet we wind up achieving the exact opposite of what we want.

When Peter joined Versity as its new chief executive officer (CEO), he quickly started to worry about all the help he needed. He could not possibly focus on all the external problems while also overseeing the company's day-to-day operations. The company had no financial plan, no health plan, and nothing in place that resembled infrastructure. Peter was convinced that if he was going to address all the company's marketing, public relations, and financial issues, he needed to hire managers to help with these internal organizational shortcomings.

However, Peter told the founders only that there was urgency to fill all of the open slots—chief financial officer (CFO), chief operating officer (COO), vice president (VP) of business development, VP of marketing, VP of engineering, VP of human resources, and executive assistant. He did not explain why he needed to hire all of these people. Anytime Peter told the founders about the problems he was observing with the company, they got upset. So, instead of focusing on the problems that he needed to hire people to solve, he focused on the people that he needed to hire.

Privately, though, Peter worried greatly, not just about all the problems the company had but about the fact that he had to work with a group of young founders who did not understand the magnitude of the problems they faced. Still, he said nothing, keeping his concerns to himself.

To complicate matters further, the founders didn't like most of Peter's hires, perceiving that they lacked technical savvy and any understanding of the college market. But the founders too were very cautious about what they said to Peter. They had brought Peter into the company because he was supposed to know more than they did about decisions like whom to hire and when to do it. They respected Peter. Still, they wondered why he was hiring so many people so quickly, especially when none of them seemed well qualified for the job. To the founders, Peter's sense of urgency about bringing in professional managers raised questions about his ability to truly understand and lead their type of company. Instead of sharing their concerns, however, they just watched, worried, and hoped for the best.

As a result of all this silencing, the founders were left unaware of all the shortcomings Peter saw in their organization, and Peter was left unaware of the founders' doubts about his new hires. Worse yet, Peter felt resentment toward the founders for not understanding his concerns about the company, and the founders started to question Peter's ability to run the company.

SILENCING SELF

By definition, when we silence ourselves, we have a perceived difference with another person; we don't, however, explain ourselves so that the other person understands our perspective. Silencing self is a choice we make—consciously or unconsciously—to not fully express our perspective. Silencing self can take place in both directions in the hierarchy: subordinates may silence themselves with their bosses, and bosses may silence themselves with their subordinates. Peers too may silence themselves with one another.

The Subordinate Sits Silently

Sam was an associate at a preeminent investment bank. He did not think his boss, a managing director (MD) at the bank, was advising their client well. The client was the CEO of a chain of fast-food restaurants who was in the process of acquiring a second chain of restaurants. Sam was one of ten associates working on the deal. The associates were responsible for collecting and analyzing the data that the MD had used to approve the proposed acquisition price. Sam, however, was convinced that the price was not fair; in fact, he thought it was a terrible price. The numbers showed that the CEO was significantly overpaying for the acquisition. But Sam and the other associates would never tell this to their boss. Questioning their boss would only cause him to have a negative perception of them. As Sam explained, "It may sound totally egotistical, but if you differ from the MD you will be perceived as less intelligent."

Since Sam never said anything to his boss about what he thought was best for their client, his boss never knew that Sam's opinion differed from his own. In other situations, a boss may question something a subordinate has said or disparage the work produced. In response, if the subordinate chooses to silence himself, he again implies to his boss that he has come to agree.

Maria was a project manager at a well-respected management consulting firm, where she had worked for more than five years. Late one afternoon, Max, the partner in charge of Maria's current project, told her that he had just looked over the presentation she had spent the past month preparing for the client.

"The presentation does not communicate the right message," he sternly informed her. Maria knew that the presentation still needed some final touches, but she certainly did not think it was totally wrong. However, she did not share her reaction with her boss. She just sat quietly, listening to his perspective, and agreed to rework the entire presentation according to his specifications. He was the partner, and because of that she believed she was supposed to do as he said, voicing no resistance. That was the way she perceived things were to be at her consulting firm.

The Boss Bites His Tongue

Bosses, too, silence themselves with their subordinates. Bosses have power inasmuch as they can punish uncooperative subordinates. But exerting formal authority may cause matters to get worse, not better.

That was Morris' concern. A faculty member at a midwestern university, Morris had been assigned a new secretary, Debbie. Early on, Morris asked Debbie to type up a set of notes he had written. The document, only a couple of pages long, came back full of typos. Later, Morris asked Debbie to scan a document and then proofread it for accuracy. This document also came back full of mistakes. When Morris asked Debbie to be more careful, she took the document back, corrected a few of the many errors, and returned it to him. Morris did not bother to give it to her again; it was clear to him that it would be faster to do it himself.

Morris quickly concluded the same thing about buying airline tickets. Several times he handed Debbie a printed itinerary, and each time she managed to get something wrong. Once it was his destination, another time the dates, and most recently the fare. In each case, she had an excuse.

Morris feared that criticizing Debbie's performance would

only make matters worse. He suspected that saying something would make her resentful and therefore make her work deteriorate even more. So he said nothing. He did not want to alienate her, and he did not have the authority to fire her.

When it came time for Morris to give Debbie feedback for her annual performance review, he still said nothing about her errors. Instead he gave her mildly positive feedback. Why? Because he feared that if he did otherwise, she might become even less helpful. By not saying anything, however, he lost the opportunity to help her to improve.

Performance appraisals are meant to provide information to employees about how well they are doing and about how they can improve their performance. Such critiques cannot, however, fulfill their purpose unless they provide clear and honest feedback. Yet, like Morris, many managers feel uncomfortable giving negative feedback. As a result, the feedback provided is often distorted and less helpful than it could be, thus undermining the review process and the employee's potential contribution.[1]

Keeping the Peace with Peers

People also silence themselves with their peers—those who have no formal authority over them and whom they have no authority over. Ted and John, two colleagues working for a publishing house, were focused on the upcoming launch of a new book. Ted, the creative designer, and John, the marketing representative, met with the rest of their team to decide the design for the book jacket. Ted had been deeply engrossed in designing the jacket. He was clearly excited about the jacket he'd created and was convinced that it suited the book perfectly. Enthusiasm was written all over his face as he presented his design to the rest of the group.

On seeing the design, John forced a smile, but underneath he cringed. He was convinced that the jacket would never sell any books. Uncertain as to what to say or how to say it, John opted to say nothing.

As the publishing season progressed, the book's jacket was printed in the catalog. It was also posted on Amazon.com. Then, as the book was about to be printed, there was a major sales conference to present the book to the sales representatives responsible for selling it. When John presented the book jacket, as he feared, the sales representatives echoed his concern—they felt they could never sell the book with its current jacket.

Having to change the jacket at this late stage created endless problems for the publisher and for Ted. The catalog had the wrong jacket in it—and it was too late to change that. Moreover, a new jacket needed to be designed immediately. All of these last-minute crises did not reflect well on Ted. Because John had hidden his early aversion to the book jacket, Ted ended up suffering, and so did the book's marketing campaign.

SILENCED BY ANOTHER

Often silencing occurs because we decide that it's best not to express a difference. However, when a person we perceive to have power over us, such as a boss, says or does something that puts pressure on us to be silent—for example, when we ask a question or voice an opinion, and in response the other person signals that we should say no more—we are being silenced by another. The signals sent can be explicit or more subtle and indirect. Being silenced by another comes in two forms—suppressing and glossing.

Suppressing

In suppressing, people convey that someone else's suggestion, recommendation, advice, or perspective is not welcome.[2]

Although suppressing can happen among peers, it most commonly occurs when managers pressure employees to do something. In response, employees silence themselves, making it seem as if they agree with their managers when, in reality, they don't.

Amar was a product development manager overseeing a team of software engineers who had committed to deliver a certain output to their boss's boss within a month. However, Amar's boss, Brian, had just okayed a change in the development process that would slow them down substantially. Amar was convinced that the change made absolutely no sense if they cared about meeting their deadline. However, when Amar told Brian exactly that, Brian dismissed his concern. Moreover, Brian told Amar in no uncertain terms that the change was not open for discussion and that Amar was never again to say anything to anyone about it. At this point, Amar lost much respect for Brian, doubting Brian's ability to manage his own boss as well as Brian's understanding of the technical issues underlying the project he was supposed to be managing. However, fully aware that Brian would write his performance appraisal and therefore influence his annual raise and potential promotion, Amar said nothing more.

Amar received explicit direction from his manager about how to handle their difference of opinion. Sometimes, however, the person in power can be less direct and yet still send a clear message as to what is expected. Rachel was the director of the counseling center at a small liberal arts college. For the past five months, she had been treating Ed, a senior in the biology department, for depression. He had been doing well in school and was deeply engaged in his senior thesis when suddenly his symptoms increased to the point that he needed to be hospitalized. Aware of how detrimental lost time in the lab would be to Ed's senior thesis, and aware that despite his severe depression he could still function productively enough to continue his lab work, Rachel agreed to take responsibility for Ed's well-being a few hours each day so he could come out of the hospital to work in the lab.

When the provost of the school learned of this arrangement, he expressed great concern to Rachel about the school's legal liability if Ed harmed himself while out of the hospital. Rachel, who was concerned most of all about Ed's well-being, felt that Ed would be in much greater danger of doing harm to himself if he were prohibited from going on with his lab work, which was crucial to his graduation and acceptance into medical school. She outlined for the provost all the precautions she was taking to ensure Ed's safety and well-being. Nothing further was said about the issue.

In subsequent staff meetings, however, the provost ignored Rachel's comments. When she spoke as a student advocate, he wouldn't look at her, and he would proceed as if she hadn't spoken. Although the provost never said anything directly to her, Rachel got the clear message that her views as a student advocate were not valued or wanted, and so she stopped sharing them.

In Amar's case, his boss made clear his desire for Amar to say no more. In Rachel's case, the provost was less explicit; his behavior, however, clearly suggested that he did not want her to advocate for the students. In neither case did the person being silenced understand the reason behind the suppressor's preferences.

Glossing

We can also be silenced by another in a more indirect way, if the other person glosses over the conflict—working past it rather than through it.[3] In glossing, the other person makes an attempt to address the conflict, but the attempt is clearly inadequate. As with suppressing, glossing over a conflict cuts off further discussion, and both parties are left without full understanding of their difference.

Jenn desperately wanted a raise. She worked for George, an

agent in a mutual life insurance company. For months, she had been mulling the situation over in her head, trying to muster up the courage to have a conversation about her salary. Then George decided to hire another person, who would be Jenn's assistant. When he suggested the idea, Jenn thought it sounded great. She also knew that this was the critical moment she had been waiting for—the moment she would ask for a raise. After George finished describing his plan and Jenn had asked a few questions, she threw in one more: "So will this new arrangement come with an increase in pay?" George, caught off guard, answered, "I think we already have a good deal." Jenn heard him out but then found the courage to tell him that she was struggling financially and that the numbers were not adding up. After he listened to her lay out her case and explain what the salary and commissions were amounting to, George muttered, "Okay, you're right. Hmmm."

After a moment of thought, he suggested, "Maybe we can have a step system, so next year, if we earn over $500,000, you can have a higher percentage of the commissions." He continued, "I'm not greedy with my money. I really am willing to share."

Jenn later noted, "George says all the right things and even indicates a willingness to address the problem. But he is not really willing to change anything." She explained that it was almost certain that the step system would amount to no increase in her pay. Asked how she would respond to George, Jenn said in despair, "I don't really know. It is hard for me to tell him anything more. He thinks he is addressing my problem."

George had glossed over the difference with Jenn. He made a superficial modification to his system for rewarding her that neither effectively addressed the underlying inequity that was bothering her nor helped her understand why the inequity existed. What George did—providing an inadequate solution—can be thought of as "patching a difference." Although the change did not address the real issue, the fact that any change was made at all compounded Jenn's difficulty in discussing the problem further with George, because to do so would require first challenging the inadequacy of the patch itself.

Sometimes, instead of patching a difference, one party may offer an explanation that is meant to mitigate the severity of the issue or to talk the other party out of the conflict—what can be thought of as "smoothing over a difference." Kate had recently moved to Vietnam as the director of a new program for an American-based nonprofit organization. When Jessica, Kate's boss in the organization's New York headquarters, had told Kate what her salary would be, Kate had realized it was the bare minimum that she could accept but had figured that the organization was reputable and that there was no room for negotiation.

When Kate started her job, however, she learned that her deputy director was making substantially more money than she was—and he knew it, because the books were open to both of them. Stunned that her new organization would take advantage of her in this way, Kate was uncertain what to do. She knew that if she said nothing, a year of hard work would pass and she would be resentful. However, she was also new to the job and the organization and wanted to make a favorable impression. Finally, Kate decided to broach the pay discrepancy with her boss. Jessica, however, quickly dismissed it as something based on "salary history." In other words, Jessica tried to "smooth over the difference," suggesting that it had a simple, logical explanation, thereby trying to make it seem unimportant and therefore requiring no further discussion.

Kate couldn't believe that her organization could be so foolish in establishing pay. She didn't care whether it was a matter of salary history or not; she was paid significantly less, her second in command knew it, and it was causing tension in their relationship. Still, Jessica's explanation made it difficult for Kate to say anything more. To do so would have required her to challenge her new boss.

Another familiar form of glossing occurs when people indicate they will do something but they have no intention of doing so—what can be thought of as "making empty promises." Having learned that a handful of associates at his law firm were complaining about sexism, racism, and overwork, Tim, the presiding partner, set up an offsite meeting with the other partners to discuss these issues. During the meeting, Tim explained the charges being made against the partners by the associates. One by one, the partners denied the accusations, and several partners complained that they were wasting a Saturday morning on issues that were of no concern to them. One, in exasperation, snapped, "Who [cares] about the associates? Look at our P&L [profit and loss statement]."

Despite the disdain, Tim urged the partners to talk to the associates. A meeting was arranged, and several partners told the associates that they wanted a harmonious office, that they wanted to encourage people to voice their concerns, and that they believed some of the issues aired were perceptual rather than actual. The partners attributed any communication problems to their own excessive travel schedules. One of the partners tried to placate the associates, saying, "I want you to know that we are profoundly interested in you as people and in your careers. We will be meeting with you monthly to discuss your career goals." The associates, however, sensed that the partners were proposing changes they had no intention of making; in other words, they were "making empty promises" to avoid confronting conflict. But, as with other forms of glossing, the associates felt there was no room for them to say anything more. Instead, several of them left the firm in the coming weeks and months.

In the case of both suppressing and glossing, one person

puts pressure on another to accept a particular viewpoint, perspective, or idea. And the result is much the same: silencing occurs, preventing the achievement of mutual understanding.

THE VICIOUS NATURE OF
SILENCED CONFLICT

Each act of silencing—whether from silencing on our own or silencing in reaction to something someone else says or does—further makes us all the more likely to silence next time. We get stuck spinning in the "silent spiral," where each act of silencing increases the likelihood we'll silence again next time, and at increasingly high cost for ourselves, for our relationships, and for the work. Understanding how this can happen and how to avoid it are what this book is all about.

CHAPTER TWO

Why the Rules of the Game Favor Silence

WHY DON'T golfers speak while their partners are putting? Why don't employees march into their managers' offices and demand a raise? Because implicit rules govern how we act in such situations. There are shared, acceptable standards of behavior that let us know what's considered appropriate and expected of us in certain circumstances. For the most part, these rules or norms are neither written down nor made explicit. They refer to the proper forms of interpersonal behavior we learn as part of becoming a member in good standing in our organizations, groups, and relationships.[1]

There are norms for all types of interactions.[2] Of particular relevance to the topic of this book are norms pertaining to whether we silence our differences or express them.[3] This chapter describes some key types of norms that influence silencing behavior and then moves on to consider the power of these norms over us, as well as our power, ultimately, over them.[4]

NORMS THAT SILENCE

Organizations have norms about what members must say and not say to fit in.[5] These norms encourage or discourage innovation and risk taking. They govern how people who speak up are treated and how mistakes are handled. People start to learn these norms as soon as they enter an organization and continue to learn them throughout their employment.

Organizations have different norms about approaching conflict. For instance, one study found that in bureaucratic organizations, executives were expected to handle conflict with subordinates unilaterally, simply by ordering them to obey—thereby suppressing them. Subordinates in these organizations were expected to silence themselves in response. In contrast, in "flatter" organizations, in which there were more top-level executives, everyone was expected to avoid differences rather than express them. In other words, in these flatter organizations, everyone—not just subordinates—silenced themselves; there was a norm of using little suppression at any level.[6]

Organizations also have different norms about recognizing and valuing differences. Research on cultural diversity has found that companies that focus on equal opportunity, fair treatment, and recruitment, and that act in compliance with federal Equal Employment Opportunity (EEO) requirements, expect everyone to be treated the same.[7] The implicit assumption is that even though people are demographically different, they don't think or act differently. This perspective focuses so much on instilling the idea that "we are all the same" that it puts pressure on people to make sure important differences are kept quiet. To express a difference is to go against the norm that we are all the same.

In contrast, companies that focus on learning from one another's differences emphasize airing and explaining different points of view and intentionally deliberating about whether and how these views should inform the work. Instead of believing that people are supposed to be just like one another—and therefore pressuring people to silence any differences—these organizations take the perspective that people are different and that expressing their differences will be beneficial. In these organizations, the norm is to speak up, expressing difference rather than silencing it.

Imagine three people sitting in a conference room deliberating over a new product, with one team member privately differing from the other two on how she thinks the group should proceed. In a company that emphasizes everyone being the same, she will likely feel pressure to keep quiet, reasoning that something is wrong with her way of thinking. In contrast, in a company that emphasizes learning from one another's differences, this same person will likely feel compelled to voice her viewpoint—recognizing it as an opportunity to promote learning and feeling comfortable that others will see it that way as well.

Quite often, norms that inhibit expressing difference stem from organizational policies or practices, such as the incentive system. When promotions or bonuses are based on the boss having a positive impression, employees often fear that raising too many questions or dissenting viewpoints will hurt the boss's impression of them, so they decide to keep quiet. As a senior analyst at an investment bank explained, "It comes down to the hierarchical nature of the bank. Basically you're just trying to make the person above you love you so you'll get a big bonus. If you start raising uncomfortable questions and being holier than thou, you may be absolutely right, but you shoot yourself in the foot. What the managing director says, goes." A *Dilbert* cartoon poignantly expresses this idea. Dilbert asks, "If we know our senior executive is making a bad decision, shouldn't we tell her?" The Boss responds, "Hmmm, yes. Let's end our careers by challenging a decision that won't change. That's a great idea."[8]

In many organizations, disagreement with authority, or "rocking the boat," is seen as a violation of company loyalty.[9] To be a loyal employee requires one to accept corporate values, policies, and decisions, never challenging them. To differ with authority or question corporate views is perceived as risky for one's career.

To complicate matters further, mixed messages are some-times sent. People are asked for an honest opinion, while orga-nizational norms warn them not to dissent. Todd worked at a large advertising firm that had been rocked by a downturn in the advertising market and by the departure of several of its key executives (and therefore key accounts). Several rounds of lay-offs had followed. The pervading atmosphere was one of inse-curity and paranoia. People were afraid they might be the next to go.

In response to all the tension about the layoffs, the manage-ment team decided to organize monthly companywide meetings. During these hour-long meetings, all the employees would gather in the conference room; food and alcohol would be served, and music would be playing. These meetings were billed as "open forums." At every meeting, the CEO would stand before the employees and praise the strength and talent of their creative teams. Then he'd show everyone recent ad pitches the creative people had put together. The CEO would also announce promotions that had taken place that month. At the end of each meeting, the CEO would invite people to speak or ask questions. A few people would ask simple questions about the progress of new ad campaigns or about administrative changes. No one, however, would dare to ask the big questions on everyone's mind: What was the future of the company? Were their jobs secure? As Todd explained, voicing any real opinions or asking penetrating questions about the health of the company would have been "sacrilegious," given the feel-good nature of the pro-gram.

It is interesting to recognize how events are often staged to ensure that the tough questions are *not* asked. Instead of addressing the real issues head on and allaying fears—or at least acknowledging the concerns of employees—management sig-nals that despite the request for questions, no one is really sup-posed to ask them. Underlying management's words requesting openness are the shared expectations about how things work at the company and what is valued and rewarded. Organization norms have a powerful influence on people's perception of what they should say and therefore on what they do say. All too often, managers with all good intention gather employees for an "open forum" while at the same time, existing norms inhibit employees from expressing their concerns.

Groups also have norms about whether and how members should respond to differences. Julian went through Ranger School, an intensive course in the U.S. Army demanding grueling physical activity and little sleep or nourishment. The soldiers within each squad (eight to ten people) quickly become a united team. One day while Julian's squad was out on a mission, the instructors found that someone in the squad had hidden some of the ammunition in a field locker to avoid carrying it. When the squad got back to camp, the instructors lined up the members and demanded that the person who had hidden the ammunition come forward and take responsibility for doing so. No one did. Julian knew full well that Gary had done it, and he suspected that others in the squad knew as well. Yet no one said a word. Julian expected Gary to step forward and was surprised when he did not. However, Julian wasn't about to risk getting a reputation for turning in a buddy. Even though they would all share the punishment if no one told on Gary, Julian perceived that as better than risking his reputation as a loyal team member. As Julian explained, "All you have is your buddies, and if you violate them, you have nothing."

Members of close-knit groups like Julian's are particularly prone to silencing themselves in keeping with the rest of the group. No one wants to be the dissenter. No one wants to voice concerns or point out potential problems because no one wants to risk being ostracized or otherwise punished by the group.[10]

Within the constraints of such group and organization norms, interpersonal norms further get established. In relationships, patterns of behavior develop—often patterns that are specific to the relationship.[11] Over time, each person comes to expect that the other will act in certain ways.[12] When two people don't open up about their differences, they establish a pattern of not doing so, and each comes to expect a continuation of that pattern from the other.

Steve had just graduated from law school and had been assigned to work with Chris, a senior partner at his new law firm. Even though Steve had heard that Chris was very demanding as a boss, he was excited about the opportunity to learn directly from a senior partner.

The first time that Steve wrote a legal memo for Chris, he worked extremely hard on it, finishing it long after midnight. Several days later when he found it in his mailbox—covered in red ink—Steve was distressed and wondered what he had done wrong. He typed in all the corrections Chris had made but did not understand the reasoning behind them. Steve, however, did not ask Chris to explain. He knew how busy Chris was and figured his "stupid" questions were not worth Chris's time. The next memo Steve wrote came back the same way—in his mailbox covered in red ink. Again Steve did not understand why, nor did he ask. This happened over and over throughout the course of Steve's first year at the law firm. As a result, Steve came to expect that no matter what he did, he would get the memo back covered in red ink. And Chris came to expect that Steve would do an unsatisfactory job that he, Chris, would have to correct.

Neither Steve nor Chris was providing the other what he needed: Steve needed feedback, and Chris needed higher-quality output. Neither, however, said anything to the other about their unmet needs. Rather, Steve and Chris just kept acting in the same way, and the more they repeated this behavior, the more they came to expect it of each other. As their pattern became established, to act differently would have required more than just acting differently—it would have required challenging the "normal" way things had come to be done in their relationship.

PERPETUATING NORMS OF SILENCE

We are socialized from a young age to maintain the norms that guide behavior in each particular situation.[13] We fear that if we don't abide by what's considered appropriate and expected, something negative will happen; perhaps someone will get angry with us, damaging our relationship. We fear looking stupid or jeopardizing our reputation, career, or bonus. We may even be afraid of getting fired.[14] Underlying most of our fears is the fundamental fear of being rejected by the other person or the group.

Just how big our fears are depends on the situation in which we find ourselves. For instance, in the advertising firm where Todd worked that held companywide meetings billed as open forums, they had already conducted several rounds of layoffs and no one knew who or how many would lose their jobs next. This situation resulted in the employees feeling anxious and insecure and made them all the more fearful of breaking norms of silence.

The magnitude of our fears also depends on who we are.[15] It matters how sensitive we are to a threat to our "face"—our image or reputation.[16] The more we as individuals fear disapproval from others, the more we will put effort and energy into ensuring that others form a positive impression of us—the more we will be attuned to what others are thinking of us and the more apt we will be to adjust our behavior accordingly.[17] When we are focused on managing impressions, we will cautiously abide by the norms that we perceive to govern the situation.

Our power relative to the other person in the relationship may also affect how much pressure we feel to abide by the norms. The more we need the other person for something we value—whether it be love, acceptance, a positive performance review, or a big bonus—the less powerful we feel.[18] And the less powerful we feel, the more conscious we will be about maintaining face and therefore abiding by the norms that govern the situation, as we perceive there is much to lose if we don't.

Where we are situated in the hierarchy of an organization or group may influence our sense of power and thus how risky we perceive speaking up and breaking norms of silence to be.[19] Such characteristics as our race and gender—identity groups that we belong to by virtue of our birth—can also play a role.[20] Take the case of a black employee who described her reaction to an incident in a staff meeting in which a white male manager expressed strong disagreement with a position that senior management endorsed: "I think that there are a lot of people who wish they could have been that outspoken," she said, "and the discussion [among black managers] was that had that been a black person, he probably would not be here today."[21]

Past acts of silencing also influence present ones, and present ones in turn affect future ones. How we are treated when we violate norms of silence and what is accomplished when we do so influence how we act. When we recognize that we have a difference with another person, we perform a mental calculus.[22] We consider the possible outcomes from speaking up and ask ourselves the following questions: What happens to people who break norms and speak up—what are the costs, and are they punished? Does anything positive happen as a result of speaking up—does anyone listen, and does anything change?[23]

In the absence of data, we tend to underestimate the benefits of expressing our differences and to fantasize about risks that have little chance of occurring.[24] We forget that norms can have exceptions. They are selectively enforced, and they are negotiated by those involved. People decide in every situation which norms apply. And we forget, too, that norms can change and that we can play a role in changing them.[25] Indeed, we also fail to recognize that not everyone—and sometimes no one—may agree that a particular norm should exist, and that therefore challenging the norm will not be nearly as risky as we presume. We also tend to expect that people won't listen to us, even though they very well might—especially if we convey our message in a clear, compelling manner.

As a result, we end up silencing ourselves, reinforcing norms of silence—the very norms of silence that we are afraid to violate and that led us to silence in the first place. Remember Max and Maria from Chapter 1? When Max told Maria that the presentation she had spent the last month working on had to be redone, she opted not to express her opinion but rather to start again. The dominant norm she sensed in that situation was an organizational norm to do as her boss said. Moreover, it was a norm many people had followed before her, with Max and with other partners at the firm. By again following the norm unquestioningly, Maria protected her own reputation as well as Max's. However, she also perpetuated the way that she and others would feel compelled to act in the future with Max and other partners at the firm.[26] Maria's act of silencing perpetuated an organizational norm of silencing. It also put in motion an interpersonal norm of silence between her and Max.

Max and Maria were engaged in a process called "sensemaking."[27] Sensemaking is well named because it means literally "the making of sense." The process entails both the *sensing* of what is happening in the context around us as well as the *making* of what is happening in that context. We go to great lengths to ensure that we abide by the norms that we perceive to govern a situation. And yet by conforming to those norms, we end up further perpetuating or *making* the norms that constrain our behavior.[28]

Beyond this self-reinforcing relationship between norms of silence and acts of silence, there are larger contextual forces that further affect this relationship—for example, authority structures, managerial practices, cultural differences, and temporal pressures may all play a role in *why* we silence in the first place.[29] However, to discuss those forces further would result in a different book. Instead, going forward, I focus on *how* the act of silencing becomes increasingly destructive to our relationships and our work and on *what* we can do to stop it. I will, though, explore in Chapter 5 why temporal pressures, in particular, can fuel this process.

CHAPTER THREE

How the Silent Spiral Works

THE SILENT spiral can begin without our even realizing it. When we silence a difference, we can manage our appearance, to make it seem as if we agree. We can try to manage our emotions to make them feel "appropriate."[1] However, despite all the effort invested in managing both our appearance and our feelings, we still cannot get rid of the unresolved difference.

When we silence ourselves, acting as if there is no difference, our difference does not disappear. Try as we might to push a difference deep inside of ourselves—so we can go on acting as if nothing has happened that might cause our relationship to derail or transform—it will not go away.

The problem is that we don't like unresolved differences. The experience of difference and the further act of silencing make us feel uncomfortable.[2] We end up blaming someone for the negative emotion or denying it exists, but the underlying discomfort does not go away. Instead, it causes us to become self-protective in our relationship, and the climate in the relationship quickly disintegrates to one characterized by distrust and fear, making us all the more likely to silence in the future.

NEGATIVE EMOTION

When we silence, we are keeping part of ourselves out of the relationship and holding our thoughts and feelings inside; this withholding can be frustrating and anxiety producing.[3] Sometimes we are well aware of this negative emotion. Doug, who worked as an analyst at an investment bank, felt it was unfair that he had to fix a major mistake in a document sent to a client. The client had called Fritz, Doug's manager, to report the mistake. Fritz in turn had informed Doug of the mistake and asked him to fix it. Doug knew the error was not his, and he did not feel it was fair that he was being asked to work all weekend to fix it. However, Doug never mentioned his discontent to Fritz— he just felt angry inside. Doug later reflected, "I felt like I could punch something. I'm not usually a violent person, but at that moment I had a physical urge to vent."

When we silence a difference, sometimes we feel anger, as Doug did.[4] Other times, we feel humiliation, irritation, frustration, anxiety, or a range of other negative emotions. Still other times, we may not be aware of feeling anything unusual because we have managed to put the feeling out of our consciousness. However, whether we are aware of our negative feelings or not, they are there, and we need to do something with them.[5]

What we often do is to blame someone else for these feelings. For example, Doug blamed Fritz for how Fritz handled the mistake. All blaming another really does, however, is allow us to convince ourselves that since others are at fault, our only option is to wait for them to change. Yet it is highly unlikely that anything is ever entirely one person's fault.[6] But, by blaming another, we avoid taking responsibility for, and control over, the situation, and nothing gets resolved.[7]

Sometimes, instead of blaming another, we blame ourselves. However, that usually turns out to be no more productive than blaming someone else. Self-blame tends to lead to self-pity and helplessness. Again, we end up taking no responsibility for dealing with the situation.[8]

Sometimes, instead of blaming another person or ourselves, we deny that the difference exists. After all, if we can convince ourselves that there is no unresolved difference, then there is no negative emotion to be felt—or so we may manage to convince ourselves. That, however, does not mean there is no negative emotion; we just aren't aware of feeling it.

Rose worked in the loan syndication department of a major commercial bank. One of her bank's major customers, Printco, had borrowed $50 million.[9] One day, a representative from Printco called the bank's managing director responsible for the loan to explain that Printco was dangerously close to defaulting on its interest payments and desperately needed extra time, via additional flexibility in their debt structure, to turn their company around.

The Printco representative claimed that the current crisis was not an indication of a larger problem but rather something short-term that the company was taking immediate action to fix. With a little digging, however, it became clear to the team at the bank that Printco's need to restructure its debt indicated much more serious trouble. Their stock price was dropping rapidly, hitting a new fifty-two-week low every day. One of the members of the team from the bank working on the deal with Printco circulated an e-mail to everyone else at the bank, laying out a long list of Printco's problems: inadequate financial tracking systems, management denial, obsolescence of a core product, and on and on.

Despite being well aware of the problems, people at the bank acted as if Printco's actions were appropriate and sufficient. However, Rose explained, for anyone who stopped to think, it was perfectly clear that Printco's actions were not going to fix its problems. Still, according to Rose, no one on her team expressed such thoughts. Rather, by perpetuating the story that the changes Printco was proposing would indeed solve their problems, Rose's team could avoid experiencing the negative emotion caused by not confronting the problems underlying this deal.

SELF-PROTECTION

There are lots of clever ways in which we can convince ourselves that the negative emotion resulting from unresolved difference is not a problem—whether through blame or denial—but as long as the difference remains unresolved, there will be an underlying sense that things are not okay. We may experience anxiety, tension, or a vague sense of discomfort; however it is experienced, it results in a greater sense of distance or disconnection in the relationship.[10] And it causes us to become more self-protective.[11]

Keith was an intelligence officer with the rank of first lieutenant in the U.S. Air Force. Because he was on a high-visibility assignment, his military base was frequently visited by important Pentagon officials as well as by members of Congress who wanted to be briefed on the latest intelligence. Keith had done extensive research and had been responsible for updating everyone on the base. However, when these high-ranking officials would visit, Keith's superior—a major—would always request that James, a captain, make the presentation instead of Keith. Keith would write the "script," multiple people on the base would ensure that it conveyed the message they wanted, and then James would deliver it. James outranked Keith, but in Keith's mind that was not an adequate reason to have James— who knew little about the situation and was new on the base— make the presentation and get all the visibility.

Keith could not make sense of why each time someone important came to visit, he was asked to stand in the back of the room—available and ready to answer any tough questions James could not handle—yet James made the presentation. Keith became progressively more frustrated, but he did not feel that he could ask for an explanation; he worried that he would appear to be self-serving if he insisted on briefing the VIPs.

Keith's disgust festered. He blamed his supervisor for not letting him make the presentations. Previously, Keith had always trusted his supervisor to manage his career, as was typical among his peers. Indeed, this was accepted as the best way to move ahead in the air force. Suddenly, though, Keith felt uncomfortable with this arrangement. He convinced himself that his supervisor did not have his best interests at heart and therefore that he could not be trusted to look out for his career. Rather, Keith perceived that he had better look out for himself, and so he resolved to take over and actively manage his own career.

When we become self-protective as Keith did, our perceptions often further become distorted. We are likely to interpret the other person's behavior through our self-protective lens, making more negative attributions about the other person.[12] These negative attributions in turn cause us to be even more self-protective because we perceive that there is more reason to defend ourselves against the other person.[13]

FEAR OF BREAKING NORMS OF SILENCE

When we feel self-protective, we become less trusting and feel less psychologically safe in the relationship—that is, we feel less safe taking interpersonal risks.[14] When we don't feel psychologically safe, the perceived risk of breaking norms of silence intensifies. We become more fearful that if we speak up, we will be embarrassed or, worse yet, rejected by the other person. If we care about preserving the relationship, we therefore become all the more inclined to abide by norms of silence.

When Maria—the project manager at the well-respected management consulting firm we learned about in both Chapters 1 and 2—silenced herself with her boss Max and agreed to completely rework the presentation they were to deliver to their client, she felt frustrated. Max and Maria had initially agreed that Maria and her team of three associates would collect two types of data—based on benchmarking and interviews. As it had turned out, they were easily able to schedule and conduct interviews, but they had struggled to find any useful benchmarking data. As Maria had become increasingly aware of this problem, she had tried on multiple occasions to contact Max. But Max was out of the country and hadn't responded to her numerous e-mail or voice mail messages. So, left on her own, Maria had decided the best way to proceed with the project was to conduct as many interviews as possible and then to prepare the presentation for the client based solely on the interview data.

While Maria clearly recognized that her team had failed to collect the benchmarking data, she had thought that they had developed a creative and quite desirable solution based solely on the interview data. However, when Max finally returned and looked over the work Maria and her team had been doing, he was greatly disappointed. He told Maria that the presentation needed to be redone. The interview data would not suffice. She would have to figure out some way to get better benchmarking data immediately.

The following week, when they presented their findings to the client based on the limited benchmarking data they were able to find, they received a lukewarm reception. Hearing the client's discontent and knowing that losing a big client like this one would have severe repercussions for his reputation at the firm, Max immediately offered to have his team do more work at no additional cost.

Now, however, there was even more pressure to perform. Because the client had been dissatisfied with their previous work, Maria and her team needed to do even more to ensure that the client would be impressed this time around. When Maria met with Max to share her proposal as to how they should proceed, again, Max disagreed with many of the details. Maria, convinced after the last client meeting that she understood the client's needs better than Max, thought his suggestions were highly problematic. She considered trying to explain to Max their downside. However, feeling more uncomfortable than ever around Max, Maria didn't want to risk being shut down again by him. Instead, she just opted to execute whatever Max believed would best satisfy the client. She'd lost so much respect for Max that she no longer cared what happened to the pro-ject—even if it hurt her own reputation.

Maria had gotten caught in the destructive "silent spiral," which begins when one does not express one's thoughts and feel-ings and ends up creating an increasingly uncomfortable and unsafe climate in the relationship that leads to further acts of silencing. Each time Maria silenced herself with Max, she became more uncomfortable, feeling less safe in the relationship, and therefore less willing to take risks and break the norms of silence—norms that already existed in the organization before Max and Maria started to work together but now had come to exist in their relationship as well.

In Part III, I'll explore ways to escape the silent spiral or, bet-ter yet, completely avoid getting caught in it. First, though, it is important to further understand how problematic it is to silence a difference. It can seem like the right thing to do at the time. Yet when we do, we start the silent spiral spinning—with all its destructive costs for ourselves, our relationships, and our work.

CHAPTER FOUR

The Costs of Saying Yes When You Mean No

E ACH TIME we silence conflict, we hinder our ability to perform the task at hand. And as the silent spiral spins, we do more and more damage to our relationships. Ultimately, we destroy our desire and ability to effectively work together.

RELATIONSHIP COSTS

Once a person gets caught in the silent spiral, unexpressed negative emotion festers. Sometimes negative feelings become so intense that we want out of the very relationship we silenced our differences to preserve. At some point, one additional act—even something insignificant that may not even relate to the original difference—may tip us over the edge. Suddenly we can no longer tolerate remaining in the relationship. Hitting the breaking point may happen rapidly, or we may be caught in the silent spiral for years, sustained by some need or desire to stay together.

When we hit the breaking point, we may exit from the relationship immediately. Sometimes, however, there are intermediate steps. There may be a sudden explosion—a burst of open conflict—which most likely will be quite destructive because of all the pent-up negative emotion. Or we may choose to remain in the relationship on a superficial level but to remove ourselves emotionally from it, to "withdraw."

Withdrawal happens when we no longer care to preserve the relationship but choose not to exit, at least not yet. It is a point beyond which we no longer bother to try to silence differences to preserve the relationship. At this point, we resign ourselves to working alongside one another, no longer trying to work together.[1]

Shoney was a research fellow who worked in a lab researching pulmonary and critical-care medicine. Praveen was a research associate (one level more senior than Shoney) who was supposed to oversee Shoney's work, helping him to think through experiments both theoretically and technically. Praveen was supposed to be there day in and day out to answer Shoney's questions and to help him to succeed. In exchange, Praveen's name would appear on anything Shoney published in the lab. The better Praveen trained Shoney and the more impressive Shoney's work was, the more benefits Praveen would reap.

Praveen was eager to maximize Shoney's productivity and constantly directed him on what to do, when, and how. Shoney would always do as Praveen told him, never asking questions or pushing back. When Shoney had first heard that Praveen was to be his mentor, he envisioned that they would work together more as partners in pursuit of knowledge than as boss and subordinate—but that wasn't the way it was turning out to be. Rather, Shoney felt that Praveen mostly just ordered him around and tried to control his every move. Moreover, Praveen frequently asked Shoney to do menial tasks around the lab, such as tagging mice they were using in their experiments, feeding them, and changing their cages. Shoney resented being asked to do these tasks, which were typically done by lab technicians. But he said nothing, doing as he was asked. Over time, however, Shoney's resentment grew as Praveen continued to treat him more like his assistant than as the competent, qualified research fellow that he was—there to learn and grow as an individual and as a collaborator.

One day, Praveen started to question Shoney about how he had spent his time the previous evening and why Shoney hadn't stayed later to ensure that the experiment was finished. Shoney could not stand Praveen's badgering any longer. He still said nothing to Praveen, but something snapped inside of him. Suddenly, he no longer cared what Praveen thought. He no longer cared to make their relationship work—enough was enough. He had hit the breaking point.

For over a year, Shoney had tried to do whatever he thought would best preserve their relationship. But at this point he became so discouraged that he briefly pondered quitting the job. He convinced himself, though, that unless he was willing to throw away ten years of climbing the ladder in medicine, he was stuck in this lab with Praveen. Even though he had little motivation or desire to keep on working, Shoney pushed himself to go back each morning. Whereas the lab was once a place in which he had eagerly spent time, hopeful that his research would make an important impact on saving people's lives, it now felt more like a chore. He had entered the final stage of the silent spiral—withdrawal—convinced that the best he could do was work side by side with, but separately from, Praveen. They were still cordial to each other, but they made no effort to work together.

A clear example of their new way of working in this state of withdrawal was seen in their next work assignment. Both Shoney and Praveen were doing independent projects with mice. If they had been working together, they would have had multiple opportunities to combine their work so that one person could care for all of the mice. Two people were not needed. There were also many potential benefits to be gained from exploring what each of them was learning and how it might be interrelated, as well as from collaborating on further tests with their mice. But Shoney and Praveen kept their mice separate, and each proceeded to do their tasks independently, creating much redundancy and no learning across their projects. As their relationship disintegrated, so too did their ability to work together.

PERFORMANCE CONSEQUENCES

As Shoney and Praveen's case illustrates, silencing conflict not only can lead to a breakdown in the relationship, it can also have negative consequences for the work. Shoney learned little from Praveen throughout the year, and in the end, they kept their projects separate, creating redundancies and preventing the benefits of two minds working together. Shoney's motivation to do the work was also profoundly affected. Indeed, when our work relationships are marked by pent-up frustration, our work suffers. And, we feel distress about ourselves and our relationships.

Lack of Motivation and Disengagement

One of the costs of silencing conflict is to our motivation and engagement. When we are in a relationship in which we don't feel comfortable speaking up, we end up feeling anxiety and negative emotion, and it is hard to be motivated as a result. In relationships in which we silence ourselves, we don't get a sense that we are worthwhile or valuable. We don't feel that our perspective matters. And when we don't feel valued, we don't experience a reason to put much of ourselves into our job or to go above and beyond the call of duty. Instead, we may lose interest in our work and start to disengage from it and our organization—psychologically, at first, and then often physically, by quitting.[2] This is highly costly for both individuals and organizations.[3] Individuals don't have the positive experience of finding meaning in and feeling passionate about their work, and the organization is not as effective as it could be; moreover, the costs of turnover can be quite high.

Lost Creativity and Learning

When we silence conflict, we may also hinder our ability to be creative and to learn in the process.[4] Had Shoney and Praveen shared insights and knowledge about their research on the mice, they might have devised some innovative tests, as well as new techniques to use in running these tests. But all of this potential was lost when they stopped sharing with each other.

Creativity involves developing novel, useful, or valuable ideas.[5] It requires divergent thinking that breaks away from established ways of doing things. Divergent thinking involves stepping outside of traditional boundaries and looking at something in a new way.[6]

We all have the potential to generate novel ideas and to engage in divergent thinking, even if we have never fully tapped into our creative potential.[7] But there are barriers that prevent us from doing so. One of the most important of these barriers is anxiety. When we are anxious, our creativity is dampened.[8] Creativity requires an environment that lets us be ourselves and feel comfortable in taking risks. Without such an environment, creative thoughts and ideas are not likely to flow. When we are caught in the silent spiral and feeling the anxiety and fear that go along with that, we are likely to generate fewer innovative ideas.

Moreover, creativity entails not just developing novel ideas but also expressing them. When members of a group express their different ideas, they have the potential to think in new ways and to arrive at solutions that are more creative than any one person could generate alone.[9] However, to reap the benefits of such potential synergy requires that people feel comfortable expressing their differences.

Jean, the director of a unit within a large not-for-profit organization, went through great effort to convince her boss to hire Melanie for a management position in her unit. Once hired, as

Jean predicted, Melanie proved to be an excellent addition to the organization. Jean and Melanie were able to work together and to invigorate several programs with fresh and creative initiatives.

However, after a while, Jean found that she would frequently receive calls from her boss, Tom, interrogating her on what she and Melanie were doing and why they weren't doing what Melanie wanted. Jean often found herself on the defensive with Tom in a relationship that had formerly been quite positive. Only later did Jean discover that Melanie had been in frequent contact with Tom because Melanie was trying to impress Tom with her great ideas so that he would promote her to a new position he was creating.

In the meantime, Jean began feeling increasingly anxious about opening up with Melanie. However, by protecting herself and not sharing with Melanie, Jean ended up inhibiting their collaboration. Not only did Jean's behavior adversely affect the relationship climate that had previously enabled such high levels of creativity, it limited her and Melanie's access to information they needed to effectively generate new ideas.

Moreover, the silencing of difference not only affects current performance with a given task, but it can also affect learning. Learning involves creating new knowledge by exploring new problems or solutions and linking ideas in new and different ways—that is, it requires effectively pushing the boundaries of knowledge.[10] An organization or group learns when its actions have been modified as a result of new knowledge or insight.[11] If no one expresses their thoughts, insights, or ideas people will likely continue thinking and behaving in the same way, and nothing will change.[12] Problems are likely to persist and may even grow worse because corrective actions are not taken.[13]

And, not only does group and organization learning suffer when conflict is silenced, but so too can individual learning. Take the case of bosses who do not provide honest feedback to their subordinates. Feeling uncomfortable giving negative performance feedback and not wanting to hurt or upset an employee who under-performs—or even one who performs well but could still improve—bosses are often not forthright about their perceptions of employees' performance. Yet, when bosses are not honest with their employees, employees are not given a chance to improve.[14] And, the same is true when subordinates are uncomfortable sharing their reactions or information with their bosses; it is costly to the other person and prevents them from being given an opportunity to adapt and improve.

Poor Decision Making

Silencing conflict not only limits the potential for creativity and learning but can also result in poor decision making. The withholding of information, perspectives, or points of view can profoundly affect the decision making process. Jerry Harvey, an organizational scholar, tells the story of the "Abilene Paradox" to illustrate one way decisions can go awry.[15] The story comes from Harvey's own experience on one hot Sunday afternoon in Coleman, Texas, while he was visiting his in-laws. It was 104 degrees, and Harvey, his wife, and her parents were on the back porch trying to keep cool by sitting under a fan, drinking lemonade, and playing dominoes. "Let's get in the car and go to Abilene and have dinner in the cafeteria," his father-in-law suggested.

Abilene? Harvey wondered. It was fifty-three miles away, and their car had no air-conditioning. "Sounds like a great idea," his wife said. "I'd like to go. How about you, Jerry?"

Thinking he should be a good husband and son-in-law, Harvey said, "Sounds good to me. I just hope your mother wants to go." "Of course I want to go," his mother-in-law chimed in.

Harvey and his family got into the car and headed to Abilene. The trip was brutal. They drove through a dust storm, which caked their sweat-soaked clothes with dust. The food at the cafeteria was terrible. Four hours later they returned hot and exhausted. Harvey describes what happened when they returned home:

We sat in front of the fan for a long time in silence. Then, both to be sociable and to break the silence, I said, "It was a great trip, wasn't it?"

No one spoke.

Finally my mother-in-law said, with some irritation, "Well, to tell the truth, I really didn't enjoy it much and would rather have stayed here. I just went along because the three of you were so enthusiastic about going. I wouldn't have gone if you all hadn't pressured me into it."

I couldn't believe it. "What do you mean 'you all'?" I said. "Don't put me in the 'you all' group. I was delighted to be doing what we were doing. I didn't want to go. I only went to satisfy the rest of you. You're the culprits."

My wife looked shocked. "Don't call me a culprit. You and Daddy and Mama were the ones who wanted to go. I just went along to keep you happy. I would have had to be crazy to want to go out in heat like that."

Her father had entered the conversation abruptly. "Hell!" he said.

He proceeded to expand on what was already absolutely clear. "Listen, I never wanted to go to Abilene. I just thought you might be bored. You visit so seldom I wanted to be sure you enjoyed it. I would have preferred to play another game of dominoes and eat the leftovers in the icebox."[16]

In going to Abilene, the family made a unanimous decision despite the fact that no one wanted to go. According to Harvey, this same phenomenon happens a great deal in organizations. People privately agree about the nature and/or required solution of a situation or problem, yet, to please each other, they don't communicate what they really think. The group pressure leads members to make a collective decision contrary to what they want to do, thus creating results that are counterproductive and sometimes even destructive. The costs of the faulty decision-making process in the Abilene story are relatively mild—the family members suffered an unpleasant day trip they didn't want to take. But in some cases, silencing conflict in the process of making a decision can have huge costs.

Harvey uses the Abilene Paradox to explain the Watergate scandal. Drawing from newspaper reports of the incident, Harvey shows that former Nixon White House staffers admitted to being uncomfortable with plans to break into the Democratic National Committee's offices.[17] For instance, Herbert Porter, a member of the White House staff, said in testimony before the Senate investigating committee that he had qualms about the plan but that he "was not one to stand up in a meeting and say that this should be stopped. . . . I kind of drifted along." Porter went on to say that he had drifted along "because of the fear of the group pressure that would ensue, of not being a team player."[18] Jeb Magruder (Nixon's deputy campaign director) gave a similar response to the investigating committee. He said, "I think all three of us were appalled [at Mr. Liddy's proposal to bug the Watergate]."[19] The men who agreed to the plan believed that it was a bad idea, yet in group meetings, none of them voiced discomfort or disagreement. Instead, the staff members silenced themselves, spurred on by the silence of their fellow staffers and the fear of being labeled as disloyal or not a team player. As we know, the outcome was disastrous for the Nixon administration.

In the Abilene Paradox, people privately, although unknowingly, hold a common assessment of a situation while publicly expressing a view that differs from what they each truly believe.[20] Group decision making can proceed in this same destructive way (i.e., toward outward unanimous agreement) even when the members privately hold varying positions.[21] Take, for instance, an executive team that made a unanimous decision to build a new plant in Houston. One member privately believed it would be more cost-effective to locate the new plant in South Carolina, and another believed it would be better to locate the plant in Cleveland, but neither expressed his dissenting opinion. As a result, the group prevented itself from exploring all the possible alternatives and analyzing their pros and cons, ending up "agreeing" on something that some of the members didn't really believe in.

Even if just one person in a group believes something different, by speaking up, that one person can make a big difference. A single dissenter can break the power of a majority. Not only might the content of what the dissenter provides be key to the task at hand, the simple fact that someone offers a different perspective may force the others to reexamine their positions or consider the issue differently.[22] It also makes others feel more comfortable in voicing their own opinions if someone else has already done so.

CHAPTER FIVE

The Speed Trap

THE COSTS of silencing conflict are profound. Worse yet, every time we silence, it becomes all the more likely acts of silencing will follow. The resulting dynamic is not only self-perpetuating but increasingly harmful over time—which is what makes the "silent spiral" so destructive.

And pressure to go fast only makes the spiral all the more destructive, which is alarming news, given that most of us live and work in a world in which things constantly seem to be urgent.[1] Time is viewed as a competitive advantage.[2] It's scarce. Anything that saves time tends to be cherished. People used to depend on clocks that had only an hour hand. Now we have clocks that measure tenths and hundredths of seconds and computers that measure nanoseconds, or billionths of seconds.[3] We have become accustomed to high-speed modems, Internet banking, and drive-through dining. We are admonished to "think fast, and act faster."[4] In *Faster: The Acceleration of Just About Everything*, James Gleick notes:

> *Society's in overdrive with no sign of braking. In elevators we manically smack the* DOOR CLOSE *button in the hope of saving a handful of seconds. Politicians average 8.2 sec-*

onds to answer a question. Top industries are hiring on the basis of quick wits. A buffet in Japan charges by the minute. And the most advanced cases of "hurry sickness" punch 88 seconds on the microwave instead of 90 because it's faster to tap the same digit twice. Yet for all the hustle, and all of technology's increasing speed, there still seems to be less and less time to spare.[5]

A SENSE OF URGENCY LEADS TO SILENCING

When we feel pressure to go fast, we often perceive that there is no time to express and reflect on our differences. We silence ourselves in the name of getting things done as expeditiously as possible. How many times has a deadline caused you to bite your tongue and think to yourself, "We just need to get on with it. We don't have time to worry about it now. We have to get it done."

Margaret, a senior manager at a large food processing company, was required twice a year to conduct a set of in-depth performance reviews of the managers who reported to her. She had known all week that she had to send the final reviews on Friday to the corporate human resources department. On Monday morning, she had provided her assistant, Tony, with a clear "to do" list, specifically outlining all the paperwork that she needed him to do during the week. By Friday morning, however, it was clear that Tony would never be done on time. Helping Tony would be costly for Margaret, who had a great deal of her own work to complete and would have to work much of the weekend as a result. Still, to get the work done on time, Margaret realized that she had no choice but to stop what she was doing and spend the day helping Tony.

Margaret was resentful that Tony had not been more efficient but rather had spent much of his time that week—as he tended to do—gossiping with the other assistants and talking on the phone to his friends. What made Margaret even more resentful was that as she worked hard to fill out the paperwork on Friday, Tony took for granted that it would get done on time and continued at his normal pace—doing some work, but spending much time engaged in social chatter.

Despite her desire for Tony to focus on the paperwork and help get it done as quickly as possible, Margaret decided that it was best just to do the work herself and take whatever help she could get from Tony. Since the project had to be in the outgoing Federal Express box by no later than 8:00 P.M. that evening, Margaret felt that the last thing she had time for was to try to figure out with Tony a more effective way for them to work together. And when the project didn't get done until 7:50 P.M., Margaret was just thankful that Tony had stayed around to ensure its completion.

Given the pressing deadline and the fact it was too late to make much of a difference in terms of completing the task on time, Margaret may well have made the best choice at the moment—not to discuss her differences with Tony. The problem was, however, that after the paperwork was finished, Margaret was so relieved that she still didn't take the time to sit down with Tony and try to create a more effective working dynamic. Instead, she silenced herself, saying nothing. But her resentment did not disappear. And when the same pattern recurred before the next big deadline, Margaret became all the more resentful.

Everyone is familiar with this last-minute pressure from deadlines. However, time pressure comes in many forms. A growing problem in our society is the constant pressure on more and more people to go as fast as possible on everything and often to do so with increasingly fewer resources.

In an ever-growing number of industries, being first to market is one source of such constant, intense, time-based pressure.[6] Jason was a market researcher at a large consumer products company in which time to market was viewed as critical. Jason worked on teams that conducted research studies to understand consumers' preferences. His current project involved gathering data about a new type of dog food specifically for puppies. At the start of the project, Rick, one of Jason's peers on the team, had laid out a detailed plan in which they would use veterinarians' lists of clients to recruit participants for focus groups. These groups would be asked a set of questions about the new puppy food. Jason had been unimpressed with this plan. How would they ever get the veterinarians to release their clients' names? And wouldn't it be more efficient and practical to use the company's traditional method of seeking feedback through surveys of customers and potential customers? Most of all, Jason worried that running enough focus groups to collect valuable information would be too time-intensive.

In a team meeting to discuss and finalize what data-collection method to use, Jason had suggested that they also conduct a survey in addition to the focus groups that Rick had proposed. Jason reasoned that at least this way they'd still have data to report even if the focus groups turned out to be infeasible—as he predicted they would be. After much discussion about the pros and cons of running focus groups while also conducting a survey, the team agreed to do both. Then, as the research got under way, Jason realized additional problems with how the team was attempting to conduct the focus groups. However, when Jason started to describe the problems to Rick, Rick showed little interest. Jason decided not to push because he feared that any extended discussion and reevaluation would delay the group more than they could afford at this critical time. Jason knew that other groups in the company involved with the product were waiting for the market research results to move forward on their own tasks, and he didn't want his group to be the cause of the product failing to be first to market—that would be a terrible mark against them. And so he silenced himself.

Sometimes pressure to go fast causes us to silence ourselves, as it did for Margaret with her assistant and for Jason with his work group. Other times, it may cause us to become impatient and to not listen fully or seek to understand the other person's perspective. In such instances, the pressure to go fast may cause us to silence someone else. Anne was head of a new division of health care at a public relations firm. The firm specialized in the consumer products market. Now Anne was working hard to help them expand and develop a health care practice. The president of her firm had told her she had a year to find clients. Six months had already passed, and she was feeling immense pressure.

Anne had recently made contact with a large pharmaceutical company that had expressed great interest in working with a public relations firm. This company had asked Anne to provide a proposal, telling her that they had asked three public relations firms for proposals and would choose the best among the three in two weeks' time. Anne knew that if she could win this one big client, the existence of her division would no longer be in question. The issue was how to write the best possible proposal. She immediately assigned her three most qualified associates to the project. The four of them, together, outlined what the proposal should look like and what data they needed to collect. The plan was that the three associates would spend the first week collecting the data and drafting the proposal, and then the four of them would get back together to assess what was left to do.

The associates worked day and night for the entire week, and Anne was pleased with their apparent effort and excited about the potential of such a large pharmaceutical company as their first major client. But when she looked at the contents of the proposal late Sunday afternoon in preparation for their Monday morning meeting, she was greatly disappointed. She thought that the team had organized the material in an unclear way and wondered why they had not collected many of the data they had agreed to collect. The next day she met with the three associates to give them her feedback and seek answers to her questions.

When Anne asked them why they had organized the proposal as they had, they immediately started justifying their choices. Feeling deeply anxious about winning the pharmaceutical company's business, Anne was in no mood for a lengthy discussion. She had very little time to finish the proposal, and she didn't know how to facilitate an effective conversation. Unsure what to do, she told the associates to go home and get some rest and that she would make some changes to their draft.

Anne figured she didn't have any more time to waste. If she was going to rewrite the proposal, she needed to get started immediately. She had failed to come to understand the choices of her associates—which she would only later learn were quite well thought out. Instead, she subtly suppressed the associates and took over the project herself to ensure its on-time completion.

When we feel pressure to go fast and people express a difference, we may suppress them as Anne did. A sense of urgency may also lead us to gloss over our differences with another person. For instance, a manager may feel she does not have time to deal with an issue of a subordinate, but she doesn't want to make the subordinate feel bad, ignored, or otherwise unattended to. So instead she may try to smooth over the difference, indicating that it is not a big deal, or she may make an empty promise, indicating that the problem will be addressed when she knows full well she has no intention of doing so.

Pressure to go fast not only causes people to silence themselves or to silence others, it also causes those whose differences are suppressed or glossed over to more readily accept this response. When people recognize that they themselves or someone else is under time pressure, they are more inclined to accept others' attempts to silence them. Emily was a business analyst in the nuclear power division of a large electric company that ran several nuclear reactors within the region. The engineering departments at each reactor frequently contracted with outside staffing firms when they needed additional help. A task force was set up to better assess the engineering departments' use of contractors and how the different departments might meet their needs in a more cost-effective manner.

Emily's boss, Dana, had asked Emily to look at some data on the contractors to help the task force document the current situation. Dana had indicated that this was not a high-priority project. When Emily got the data, she discovered some discrepancies in who had been hired and at what pay, but when she tried to contact the person who had originally compiled the data, she learned that the person was out of the office for a couple of weeks. Since no one else could easily answer her questions, and since Dana had given her the impression that there was no rush associated with the project, Emily put it in her "to do" pile and promptly forgot about it.

A week later, Dana suddenly rushed into Emily's cubicle and said that she needed Emily to attend a meeting later that afternoon at which several people on the task force would be discussing the contractor situation. Emily told Dana about the discrepancies she had found in the data and indicated her reluctance to attend a meeting so unprepared. Dana dismissed her concerns, saying that the discrepancies were no big deal, and explaining that the task force just wanted an opportunity to meet Emily and to understand better what she was doing.

Emily went to the meeting and quickly learned that although Dana might not have thought that these discrepancies were important, the people on the task force were alarmed by them. And they wanted to know why Emily had not taken a more active role in addressing these discrepancies sooner. Emily did what she could to fend off the attacks and justify her approach. However, mostly she just sat there in utter disbelief, hoping that the meeting would soon be over. She felt embarrassed and confused. She didn't understand how she'd ended up in this situation. Had she misunderstood Dana's directions? Had Dana misunderstood the task force's needs?

After the meeting, Emily decided she had to explain to Dana what had happened at the meeting and how much it had troubled her to be put on the spot like that. However, when Emily finally found herself alone with Dana for a few minutes, Dana quickly dismissed the issue, telling her, "There is nothing to worry about." But Emily was not convinced. She didn't think Dana fully understood what had happened in the meeting. Emily was concerned that she had made a terrible impression with the senior managers on the task force. She had been unprepared and seemingly irresponsible. She just kept replaying the meeting and the harsh words that had been tossed around. But she didn't feel she could say anything more to Dana. She knew Dana was extremely busy and sensed that Dana thought her problems were petty in comparison. Emily knew as well that she needed to get on with all that she had to do.

SILENCING DIFFERENCE INTENSIFIES A SENSE OF URGENCY

Pressure to go fast makes people all the more likely to silence their differences. And, as we saw in the last chapter, silencing differences, in turn, has negative consequences for relationships and work. Not only do people feel negative emotion that builds up inside of them, but actions occur with less input of ideas and less deliberation.[7] Lack of input and hasty deliberation can lead to an inferior decision-making process and to less potential for creativity and learning. In turn, if the task depends on divergent thinking, these less effective processes often result in problems that take time and attention to resolve. And because of the mounting work from these additional problems, the sense of urgency intensifies, and so too does the pressure to silence.

In each of the above examples, not only did time pressure lead to silencing, but the silencing itself ended up causing negative consequences that only further increased the pressure to go fast. For instance, when Margaret silenced herself with her assistant, Tony, not only did she end up working much of the weekend on tasks that she could have done on Friday, but she missed an opportunity to create a work pattern with Tony that would be more efficient and cause less stress before big deadlines in the future.

Jason's team, too, needed to move quickly in conducting the market research about the puppy food, so Jason didn't express his ideas on fine-tuning their methodology in conducting focus groups. However, the company ended up with a product that consumers disliked, when, as it turned out, they could have easily corrected the problems before launching the product had they collected valid data. Instead, they had to invest extra effort to not only fix the problem with the brand's image but also improve it even more, so it would appeal to customers who, because of the much-delayed launch of the rebranded product, now had other options. Moreover, the market research group not only had to collect data on the rebranded product but also had to complete all the new research for the next year's line of products. As a result, they felt all the more overwhelmed with everything needing to get done.

Anne's silencing herself with her three associates in response to pressure to attract as many clients as soon as possible also created even more pressure. She failed to incorporate the valuable ideas of her team of associates and ended up writing the proposal for the pharmaceutical company on her own, drawing on only her own perspective and insights. Since she and the associates never engaged in an in-depth discussion of their different ideas, they missed a chance to bounce ideas off of one another and facilitate their collective creativity. In the end, the pharmaceutical company chose a different public relations firm, which only increased the pressure on Anne and her group to find some clients quickly.

And when Dana glossed over Emily's concerns about what

had happened in the task force meeting regarding the data about the contractors, Emily felt all the less trusting of Dana's judgment and all the more pressure to make all of her tasks high priority, despite what Dana said. However, once Emily started to make all her tasks high priority, she lacked any sense of where to start and in what order to pursue her work. She quickly became overwhelmed with all she had to do.

Acts of silencing can intensify the very need for speed itself. Indeed, we can become so obsessed with responding to the need for speed that we make the need for speed so intense that it destroys our ability to work together efficiently and effectively.

Pressure to go fast can have positive benefits that we should not overlook.[8] For instance, pressure to go fast can cause individuals and companies to find new ways of working that enable more to get done in less time.[9] Such pressure can be very productive when it results in redesigning work processes so that people focus on value-added time and eliminate nonessential work.[10] When people learn to be more efficient, they may further be able to provide goods and services at lower cost to consumers.[11]

The problem, however, is that by trying to speed up work we often do not reap these types of benefits. Instead, we end up making overstretched workers feel more overstretched and managers already focused on crises all the more so.[12] In response to all the pressure, people feel compelled to silence their differences. But, problems follow. And problems only further intensify the pressure to go fast. Ultimately, the pressure to go fast and our tendency to silence in response can cause us to fall into a self-made "speed trap."[13]

THE DESTRUCTIVE SILENT SPIRAL

We've learned about the many forms of silence—silencing self and silencing others, suppressing and glossing. We've seen how acts of silence perpetuate norms of silence, which keep on perpetuating acts of silence, which only further reinforce norms of silence. And we've seen how each act of silence further causes negative emotions that create feelings of self-protectiveness that translate into increased fears about breaking norms of silence. We've also considered how acts of silence can impinge on creativity, prevent learning, lead to poor decisions, and ultimately destroy relationships. And now we've added that pressure to go fast can make people all the more likely to silence, which results in negative performance consequences and, in turn, intensifies a sense of urgency.

Part I has used a set of "episodes," or single snapshots, to help illustrate the different components of the silent spiral, why it perpetuates, and at what cost. Part II is more like scenes from a movie, the movie I saw when I spent nineteen months observing Versity from conceptualization to bankruptcy and beyond. The story of Versity helps to demonstrate how the ideas we've been exploring so far play out in real time.

Moreover, because Versity was a dot-com, the speed and intensity of the office was noticeably different from the more established Fortune 500s I had previously observed. And, its great intensity and pace allowed me to capture the cumulative damage of silencing conflict, something that would have been much harder to detect over the same period of time in a company where life proceeded at a slower pace. Indeed, being able to explore the effects of the great intensity and pace at Versity revealed where our world may well be heading if we continue to speed up our interactions as much as possible. At Versity, pressure to go fast fed the silent spiral, making the dynamic all the more vicious, and ultimately inescapable.

The story of Versity therefore poignantly illustrates how a company can not only get caught in the silent spiral but also get trapped by its own need for speed, making the costs of silencing all the more rapid and all the more destructive. Although it is tempting to attribute what happened at Versity to the dot-com world, Versity's story can teach us important lessons about the unacknowledged costs of silencing, and about the added danger when silencing happens in a world that treasures speed. In our daily lives many of us face pressure to go fast, and we end up silencing our differences in response. We need to be careful, or we too may find ourselves caught in a "speed trap" we ourselves have created.

PART TWO

The Silent Spiral in Motion

CHAPTER SIX

What Clyde and Howie Wouldn't Say

CLYDE AND Howie met for the first time over margaritas at Renee's, a Los Angeles bar.[1] It was the summer of 1998, following their junior year in college. Both were in L.A. for the summer and shared a common friend in Daniel, who had suggested that they get together.

Howie, who was working as a programmer for Citysearch, was immediately awed by Clyde's handle on finance. Tall and wiry, with short chestnut hair and dark glasses, Clyde peppered everything he said with financial jargon. Clyde was spending his summer as an analyst for the investment bank of Donaldson, Lufkin & Jenrette (DLJ). He had worked hard to land this prized internship in what he thought was to be his dream industry. His grandfather had been a successful banker, and Clyde had always planned to follow in his footsteps. Now, as Clyde described his job to Howie, there was much that he could not say because of the confidentiality agreement that he had signed with DLJ. This shroud of secrecy added to the allure of the conversation.

For his part, Clyde was also impressed by Howie's technical savvy. A little shorter, heavyset, with thick oval glasses and a cropped haircut, Howie not only looked the part of the engineer, he exuded the passion of an entrepreneur. Howie had run his own video production company since the seventh grade, taping events such as weddings and bar mitzvahs. By the time Howie graduated from high school, he had already made close to $40,000.

Most recently, with their mutual buddy Daniel, Howie had founded Notes4Free. He explained to Clyde that the vision of their company was to create a large user base of college students by providing free online lecture notes. They would make money through advertisements and through e-commerce focused on educational products (e.g., online study guides and book synopses). Howie told Clyde that in his spare time he was busy creating an intranet that would enable the internal communication and information exchange necessary to monitor notetakers and campus managers around the country.

⁓

Daniel and Aaron, Howie's co-founders of Notes4Free, were in New York City working as summer interns. Daniel was working at the New York office of DLJ, and Aaron was a programmer for DoubleClick.

One evening, late in the summer, at a dinner in honor of DoubleClick's summer associates, Aaron found himself seated next to DoubleClick's CEO, Kevin O'Connor.[2] O'Connor was worth nearly a billion dollars and thanks to the rapid growth of online advertising was one of the most powerful technology mavens on the East Coast. Aaron knew he had to overcome his natural tendency to be quiet. This was a big moment. Filled with nervous energy, he turned to Kevin and engaged him in conversation.

At first, like many of the people who heard about Notes4Free, Kevin didn't understand the concept. Where Kevin went to school there were no notetaking services. He was not familiar with students trudging down to the local note shop and paying between $30 and $50 a semester for typed copies of lecture notes. He didn't realize that lecture note services were common on major college campuses across the country. Nor did he realize just how profitable this industry was. As a result, Kevin could not relate to Aaron's enthusiasm as he described the benefits of getting class notes quickly, easily, and, best of all, for free. But Kevin finally grasped that the idea was to use the class notes to attract students to the Notes4Free website, with an ultimate goal of aggregating the college market for potential marketing purposes. Kevin told Aaron, "I like ideas, and this is a great idea. I have bucks in my sock—what will it take?" Before the evening was over, Kevin asked Aaron to stop by his office the next day.

Immediately after dinner, Aaron looked for the nearest pay phone to share the news with Howie and Daniel. It so happened that Daniel was working on a deal at DLJ that involved DoubleClick. He had seen the financial information about Kevin and DoubleClick. Bound by the confidentiality agreement he had signed with DLJ, Daniel only made it clear that this was huge.

When they met the next afternoon, Kevin told Aaron that he and his buddies had no time to waste, that they had a limited window of opportunity. Companies were quickly staking out their space on the Internet, and if they wanted to establish Notes4Free as the leader in the college market, they needed to act immediately. Kevin never said the exact words "drop out of school," but he impressed on Aaron that it would be awfully difficult for full-time students to launch a company.

స

At the end of the summer, when Howie, Daniel, and Aaron returned to Ann Arbor for their senior year at the University of

Michigan, they were returning to the area where they had grown up. They had all been part of the same Jewish youth group during high school in an upper-middle-class suburb of Detroit less than an hour from Ann Arbor.

They each decided to take only one course that fall to free up time for Notes4Free. For the next several months, they worked day and night. Yet despite endless preparations to launch their website come January, they had nothing concrete to show for all their hard work. And they had no money. In October, they decided to call Kevin O'Connor. He had previously offered financial support, and they decided it was time to follow up. Although Kevin did not say "no" during this conversation, he told them that they would be much better off if they went first to their family and friends, people who believed in their abilities and would give them the most money for the least ownership of the company.

By the time they hung up the phone, they felt awful. They could barely afford to pay their living expenses. They were putting everything they had into preparing to launch Notes4Free on the Big Ten university campuses for the winter semester. The business would be costly to operate. Notetakers were to be paid $8 for every lecture, amounting to $300 a semester per course; campus managers would make $1,500 a semester. They estimated that they needed to raise half a million dollars to make it through the winter.

Their parents could not provide much help. Howie's parents were not even speaking to him since he had basically dropped out of school at the beginning of the term. Aaron's family had recently had some business troubles of their own and had no money to spare. That left only Daniel's parents. Daniel's father was a successful doctor, but he was already supporting Daniel's mother and Daniel's two younger siblings. He very much wanted to support Daniel in whatever he did, but he could give only a few thousand dollars to this endeavor.

Meanwhile, the site made no money. But the issue wasn't really about making money. The issue was about aggregating users. It was all about getting students' eyeballs to their website—so they could show them advertisements and ultimately sell them products. Still, somehow, somewhere, they needed to get some money to pay for all of this.

With little money, no idea how they might raise it, and only a dream that somehow things would work out, Howie, Aaron, and Daniel set out to the Big Ten universities to hire students to be campus managers. The plan was for campus managers to work part-time, hiring the notetakers, monitoring the notes, and marketing the site on their respective campuses. They drove to each campus. When they arrived, they would go straight to the student union, set up a table, and start talking about their company to everyone who would listen. They promised to pay the campus managers and to provide them with stock options. And they succeeded in hiring someone at each of the seven Big Ten schools that they visited: University of Michigan, Michigan State, University of Wisconsin, University of Illinois, Indiana University, University of Iowa, and Ohio State.

꒰ꙮ꒱

Clyde, also in his senior year at the University of Michigan, was Daniel's roommate and was watching firsthand as his friends struggled to raise money for their company. Clyde had found his dream job at DLJ a big disappointment. He had come to realize he did not like investment banking. He started to envision how he could help turn Notes4Free into a successful enterprise. Clyde came from a much wealthier family in New Jersey and had money of his own. Most important, he was confident in his own abilities to pitch the company so that people would want to invest.

Clyde was different from the other three. He was not a technical visionary consumed with coming up with ideas for products. What he could add was a real obsession with money and connections. Clyde was a salesman, in the truest sense of the word. He was born to sell. In this case, what he could sell was the right to invest in this company.

In November 1998, Clyde proposed that he join Notes4Free.

If he could deliver what he promised, the three founders reasoned, Clyde would be able to help them make it through this tough period. After some negotiation, they agreed that he would be the company's fourth founder.

꒜

The first thing the founders did after Clyde joined was to choose job titles. They agreed that Howie deserved the title chief executive officer (CEO), given that he'd done most of the technical work in creating their intranet and therefore making their company possible. They decided to make Clyde the chief financial officer (CFO), Daniel the chief operating officer (COO), and Aaron the chief technology officer (CTO).

Clyde convinced the others that they needed a broader, more encompassing name for their company, a name that described what they were doing but also made them sound more substantial. They brainstormed for hours, writing down multiple combinations of *student, school, college, campus,* and *university* until they finally settled on *Versity,* short for "university." They changed the company's official name from Notes4Free to Versity.

Next they rented a suite on the fourth floor of the Key Bank building on the main street in Ypsilanti. It was roomy and cheap, about one-third of what a similar space would have cost in nearby but more upscale Ann Arbor. They were definitely not located in a great neighborhood; drug dealing was often spotted in the parking lot. Their first month in the building they were robbed. They did, however, have ample space. They had what they referred to as the "tech room," the "business operations room," the "conference room," the "supply room," and the "lounge."

Versity suddenly felt like a real company. The founders were working harder than ever and were fully committed to making their company a success. They looked around and saw other people doing it. Why couldn't they?

~

Clyde brought a new set of skills. He had the willingness and ability to pick up the phone, cold-call someone, and start describing their company with enthusiasm and conviction. By early February 1999, he had secured commitments from four angel investors and more than twenty family members and friends, for a total of $675,000.

~

Evo, a twenty-seven-year-old owner of a bricks-and-mortar notetaking service at Michigan State University, had become worried, very worried, that online notes would put his store out of business. Having heard about Versity on the evening news, he called to propose that he play a role in helping to expand the company. Having run his own business for the past six years, he claimed to have much value to add. After meeting several times, the founders offered Evo a job as their notemaster, which meant that he would manage all of the campus operations.

But as much as Evo was excited about the opportunity to join Versity, he also wanted to continue to operate his own store, selling paper copies of notes, which netted close to $150,000 each year. He did not want to lose that income. He had a wife and two children to support.

The founders viewed Evo's store as direct competition, but

since they could not pay Evo anything close to his level of income, they finally agreed that Evo could continue to work at both in the short term. They made it clear, however, that they expected him to make Versity's success his number one priority. Because Evo insisted on keeping his own company operating, they were able to negotiate a low salary and only a 2 percent ownership of Versity. Evo agreed to commute a couple of days a week from his home in Lansing (about an hour from the Versity office).

Despite some concerns about his contract, all four founders shared an enthusiasm about Evo. They trusted that he would close his store after a short while. He seemed hardworking and entrepreneurial. They viewed his knowledge of notetaking, which had taken years to acquire, as a competitive advantage that added immense value to their company. Versity did have competition in the online notes business, but the founders were convinced that none of these companies had Evo's knowledge or experience.

When Evo joined in mid-February, Versity had successfully launched at seven schools, each with a campus operations manager (COM) and ten to fifteen notetakers. Evo quickly showed great ambition, starting to plan for the fall launch. He envisioned being at fifty schools with fifty notetakers each.

A few weeks after Evo joined the company, the campus manager at Michigan State quit. Evo volunteered to take on this job on top of his other responsibilities. The founders were pleased by Evo's willingness to pitch in, but to their surprise, user numbers at Michigan State soon plummeted. Privately, Evo confessed that he was trying to keep Versity low-profile at Michigan State until he decided whether to give up running his own company there. The founders knew Evo was slacking on his responsibilities, but they didn't know why.

When COMs on other campuses began to complain that Evo was not supporting them, Clyde took action, whipping off an e-mail to Evo. Clyde told Evo that he was not adding the value that he could on the campuses and accused him of not communicating effectively with the campus managers and not working hard enough in general. Clyde demanded that Evo immediately increase his work hours and start showing better results at Michigan State.

Evo was startled. He thought he was working hard, putting in significantly more hours than he ever had before. Of course, he failed to recognize that he was now trying to work two jobs and not just one—at Versity and at his own store.

Evo convinced himself that Clyde was out of line and was upset even more that the criticism was coming from a kid. He called Howie and threatened to quit. "I'm working my ass off. Clyde is ridiculous. I've had it."

Howie panicked at the thought of losing Evo. Terrible repercussions ran through his head. People had invested because Evo was involved. They had to keep Evo. As Howie listened, he agreed that Clyde was wrong. Howie reassured Evo that he was wonderful and performing well above their expectations. Howie told Evo exactly what Evo loved to hear—how central he was to the operation and how much they valued him as a member of the team.

As soon as Howie hung up the phone, he marched into the next room and hovered over Clyde's desk. Howie tried to sound calm, but it was hard for him to hide his rage. He slowly and deliberately said, "You almost made Evo quit." His voice rising, the pace quickening, he continued, "You can't treat people like that. You almost made Evo quit. We can't afford to lose Evo. You have to apologize. You have to do whatever it takes to save this relationship."

Clyde sat quietly and listened to Howie's attack.

And then he agreed to call Evo to apologize.

ॐ

Talking to Clyde about this incident, I was surprised by how much he hadn't said to Howie. Clyde was still livid that Evo had not been working hard enough. He found Evo's behavior unacceptable and believed he was the only one who had had the courage and good sense to tell him so. Clyde believed that a company should not have people that don't carry their own weight, and this was especially true for the management team. Clyde worried about the company's culture and feared a norm of laziness might develop among its workers.

Yet Clyde voiced none of this to Howie. He simply dropped it. He placed great importance on their relationship. He knew that they needed each other to make their company a success. He worried that expressing his concerns would only waste valuable time and might jeopardize their relationship. Clyde—quietly going along despite personal reservations—*silenced himself.*

The way in which Howie had approached Clyde made it difficult for the two of them to effectively discuss their differences. Howie spoke in the heat of the moment, when he hadn't had a chance to calm down and figure out how he wanted to approach the situation. He had attacked Clyde and tried to force him to act in a certain way. He failed to try to clearly state what he believed and why, and to work to understand what Clyde believed and why. Howie did not know why Clyde had sent Evo the e-mail, nor did he try to find out. Rather, when Clyde acquiesced, Howie figured that he had resolved the matter and moved on.

Only Clyde knew what he was holding back from Howie. But it never occurred to him to approach Howie when he was less angry and explain why he thought there was a problem with Evo, or why he feared it could create problematic expectations in the future with respect to how they treated employees who lacked commitment.

The fight over Evo marked the first time I recognized a conflict being silenced at the company. It was a pivotal moment, because the relationship between Howie and Clyde was still so new and they still had much respect for each other. But by not speaking up at this early stage in their relationship and working through their differences, Howie and Clyde unintentionally made it all the more difficult to establish effective and productive interpersonal norms in their relationship. Rather, trying to get on with their work as quickly as possible, they were unintentionally setting destructive patterns in motion that would make it all the more difficult to handle similar situations in the future.

♪

Evo started having heated arguments with the founders over the value he added to the company. Without his notetaking experience, he argued, no one would come to the site. The founders thought Evo was quite important—and might even have considered raising his percentage of ownership—but they had no intention of doing so until he agreed to shut down his competing business.

♪

The founders had been incredibly successful to date. By the end of March 1999, they had six full-time employees in addition to themselves and had plans to expand to fifty schools the following fall semester. They had exceeded their initial fundraising goal. Still, they decided to meet with a few venture capitalists (VCs).

The first VC that they met with was Bud, a young associate from Robertson Stephens. The meeting started with each of them introducing himself and briefly describing his background and current set of responsibilities. The meeting continued with Bud asking pointed questions about their business plan.

After Bud left, the five of them—the four founders and

Evo—reconvened to debrief the meeting and give one another feedback. Howie was upset that they had agreed with everything that Bud had said. He thought that these VC guys were slick and that they often said things to see if people would agree. Howie argued, "We need to stand our ground and be confident in our plans. We should not be appeasing them." Howie and Clyde both felt that Daniel had undersold himself. Despite their harsh tone, Daniel welcomed the criticism and suggested that they practice over the weekend in preparation for the next meeting with a VC, scheduled for the following week. They agreed it was a good idea for them all to practice. They went on to praise Aaron for how well he had talked about DoubleClick and the relationship that he had established with Kevin O'Connor. They also talked about how the CEO of Hotmail had been referred to as "hallucinogenically optimistic" and they needed to be that way too.

In the end, Bud did not invest. He informed them that his firm did not invest in such early-stage companies. However, he was eager to stay in touch and to follow their progress.

☙

When the founders met with Craig, an associate at Piper Jaffray Ventures, he was exceedingly impressed. During his first meeting with them, he told them that Piper Jaffray would be interested in investing $200,000. If they accepted the firm's money, Craig further explained, he would be in a position to act as an advisor.

The founders particularly liked the possibility of having Craig involved. They recognized their inexperience and believed they could greatly benefit from his help. Howie told the others, "Craig is a very smart guy, and we should listen carefully to everything he says." When Craig started talking about all the people in Silicon Valley he'd introduce them to—the law firms, banks, public relations firms—they got even more excited.

ॐ

During one of his first visits to Versity, in a meeting with the four founders and Evo, Craig launched into a discussion about everyone's salary and quickly discovered that Evo was unhappy. Craig reminded the founders that Evo was a big reason Piper Jaffray had invested. "He gave us lots of confidence that he was able to take the old model and use it as a jumping-off point," Craig said.

Craig lectured the founders about the need to make everyone happy and to pay no one under market. At twenty-seven years old, Craig too was early in his career, and he desperately wanted Versity to succeed. Not focused on conserving money, he suggested that they double Evo's salary, give him more equity, and create a bonus scheme based on user numbers so he had an incentive to drive users to the site. The biggest problem for the founders was that Evo was in the room for Craig's whole lecture.

Until this visit, the founders had been eager to follow Craig's advice. Now they began to question his motives. Why did he lecture them in front of Evo? And why did he care so little about how they spent their money?

They suddenly worried that Craig was trying to make them totally dependent: the more money Craig convinced them to spend, the more money they would need to raise, and the more dependent they would become on Craig and Piper Jaffray. The idea terrified them. They called Kevin O'Connor. "Be careful," he warned them. "VCs always have their own agenda." The founders realized they had been too trusting and were determined not to let Craig run their company. It was *their* company, not his.

ॐ

In the meantime, Evo was thrilled to hear Craig tell the founders to double his salary, increase his equity, and establish a bonus structure based on user numbers. He expected these changes to be made immediately. When they weren't, he stopped working.

The founders thought Evo was being ridiculous.

Clyde called Craig to tell him how displeased they were with the way he had handled his visit and the effect it had had on Evo. Craig was caught off-guard, unaware of the trouble he had caused. When he heard that Evo was demanding a $150,000 salary and a 6 percent stake in the company, Craig agreed that Evo was demanding far too much. In a plea for forgiveness, Craig told Clyde, "I was only trying to help." After hanging up the phone, Craig wrote a long, apologetic e-mail, cc'ing all four founders.

When the founders doubled Evo's salary but kept his level of ownership at 2 percent, Evo did not come back to the office. Convinced that the founders wanted too much for too little, Evo told me, "A combination of their age, personality, and inexperience makes it impossible to work with them. They're inflexible. They simply don't understand that people won't work all of the time. They are delusional about what's involved in making a good idea a reality."

Within the week, on April 16, 1999, Evo resigned.

The founders were relieved. They had come to fear what Evo was up to.

༄

With Evo out of the way, the founders focused their concerns on Craig. He was supposed to be arranging all the meetings for a California trip that Howie and Clyde were planning. They needed to find a law firm, hire a public relations firm, and make initial contacts with potential investors for their next round of financing. They began to realize Craig was not as networked as he had led them to believe. As it turned out, they were able to set up much better meetings on their own. Craig introduced them to one "little, not so good, dumpy" law firm, while Howie's cousin helped them meet and strike a deal with Brobeck, one of the best law firms in Silicon Valley.

Both Craig and Evo were five years older than the founders. Both were expected to bring Versity much-needed expertise. The founders had had great enthusiasm about both, and yet both had turned out to be major disappointments. After those experiences, the founders became less convinced that age mattered, believing Evo offered very little they didn't already know. Note-taking, they decided, was not rocket science, but common sense. As for Craig, he had botched the situation with Evo and then had failed to come through in California. If nothing else, the founders learned that they needed to be more careful about whom they trusted.

⌁

The organization was getting bigger, and the founders wanted to maximize their employees' productivity. To Clyde, effective management meant control, order, punishment—everyone doing what he said. Howie, however, was trying to create an environment in which people enjoyed working, which he believed would make them most productive. When Howie suggested that they give people one day off a week, Clyde started detailing the long hours people worked at DLJ.

But Howie interrupted him: "This isn't DLJ. Don't ever use that as an example ever again."

Clyde didn't respond.

Howie continued, "You really don't understand how to work with people or how to manage. You only know how to order and expect results." He went on to call Clyde a "slavedriver."

Clyde disagreed: "People aren't working hard enough, and

what I'm doing is trying to create some fear to make sure things get done."

Howie just kept saying he didn't want his company to be like DLJ, but rather he wanted Versity to be a "fun, family friendly, supportive place, where people are enthusiastic about their work. Fear is not the answer. It doesn't work. It shouldn't be the way we do things around here." Suddenly noticing that Clyde was not paying attention, Howie raised his voice and snapped, "Clyde, look at me when I'm talking to you!"

Clyde snapped back, "Howie, I don't have to stare you in the eye twenty hours a day." Then, after taking a second to cool down, Clyde said, "Look, I know I'm demanding."

"You're not demanding, you're annoying."

"I'm demanding."

"No, there's a difference," Howie explained. "You can be demanding in a good way or be demanding and annoying. You really have to watch it. If you continue to badger and annoy people in this company, the repercussions will be tremendous! *Don't [mess] with me on this*. I'm growing tired of it."

At this point, their exchange came to an abrupt end. Howie sensed that Clyde still disagreed with him, but he had had enough. They didn't have time, or so he reasoned, to bicker over what the culture of their company should be. They had work to do. As CEO and convinced that he knew best, Howie perceived he had no choice but to silence Clyde.

At first, both Howie and Clyde had spoken up, but neither one had done so effectively, and in the end they silenced their conflict. The two argued, and then Howie ultimately put his foot down, never engaging the conflict constructively but instead becoming impatient and *suppressing* it. This type of silencing results not from the passivity or self-censorship of one side but from the quashing of open resistance of one side by the other. As we saw in Chapter 1, one person can pressure another to silence themselves in more and less subtle ways. In this case, Howie was explicit that he'd had enough, and in response, Clyde silenced himself.

Sometimes it is necessary for one person to make a decision even if another disagrees. Indeed, sometimes that is the only way to move forward with a decision. However, before reaching that point, it's valuable for each person to try to understand the other person's perspective. Often, in the process of seeking mutual understanding, a solution that both people can agree on will emerge or can be found through some additional creative thinking. But Howie and Clyde did not attempt to go down this path. Neither perceived he had the time to try to understand what the other was thinking or why.

Moreover, when Howie responded to Clyde's statement that he desired Versity to be like DLJ, he failed to take the time to calm down first so that he could approach the conversation in a constructive way. Instead, he launched into a heated set of personal attacks, even threatening Clyde at one point. He also jumped to conclusions about what he thought Clyde wanted, without trying to find out whether those conclusions were based on well-founded assumptions. Howie might instead have asked Clyde what about DLJ he aspired for Versity to be like, how many hours he wanted people to work, and why he thought that would be beneficial for their company. Getting answers to these questions would have enabled Howie to better understand where Clyde was coming from and why—and ultimately would have enabled him to make more accurate assessments about what Clyde had in mind.

Although Clyde had been explicitly suppressed by Howie, he too still could have tried to do something about it. To do so, however, he would have had to force himself to try to understand what was beneath Howie's hostility. Clyde also might have pointed out to Howie that Howie was silencing him and that this was an important issue that needed joint exploration. Clyde further could have presented his own reasons for wanting Versity to be like DLJ and could have offered Howie the opportunity to ask questions as well as explain his own goals for the company and his values in terms of managing its employees.

Instead, neither Howie nor Clyde took responsibility to explore their differences and what was behind them. The result was discontent on both sides: Clyde resented that Howie had dismissed his opinion; Howie found Clyde unreasonable and resented his unwillingness to back down on his own accord.

Clyde's bitterness further led him to bigger questions about Howie's competence as a manager. To motivate people, Clyde reasoned, you need to always be aware of what they are doing, give them close supervision, and show that you take an interest. Howie, in the meantime, had become increasingly disgusted with how Clyde wanted to run the company. The trust and respect they had once had for each other was being undermined.

If Howie and Clyde had been more adept at recognizing their differences and more knowledgeable about why it was so important to address them and how to do it most effectively, they might instead have engaged in a constructive discussion that would have enabled them to find more productive ways of dealing with the situation. What could have been an opportunity to make their relationship more effective and to reach a new and possibly improved understanding of their management task instead further set in motion a pattern of silencing that was becoming increasingly destructive to their relationship.

჻

Despite these struggles, everyone at Versity remained tremendously committed to the success of their company. They were one another's friends and family, working and living together, socializing and celebrating one another's birthdays. Their energy and enthusiasm abounded. Everyone was working all the time and sacrificing anything else that might be going on in their lives in order to build the company. Howie had a metal container full of caffeinated mints that he often handed out when he walked around the office. He half joked, "These Penguin caffeinated mints are keeping the office alive."

ॐ

To realize their current plan for expansion, the founders estimated that they would need to raise $10 million in the next round of financing. They were planning to raise venture capital. In early June, Clyde called a meeting because he wanted to be sure that they were all clear about what that would entail.

Clyde began, "We will have to give up equity in the company. Currently we own about 66 percent, but after this round, we collectively will own less than 51 percent." To appeal to the top-tier VCs, Clyde was convinced that the founders had to signal their willingness to give up their management positions.

Howie, however, was deeply conflicted about giving up his role as CEO. He explained to the other three, "It is clearly important that we be *willing* to give up our positions, but I don't think we should invite it openly. We should not just do what the VCs want. It has to be the right thing to do for the company." Howie thought that they should promote their age not as a liability but rather as their greatest asset, because it uniquely qualified them to understand their market. He asserted, "We are geared to college students, and we are just recently college students. We know about the market. It would not be a good move to just stick anyone in that role, even if they do have more experience managing."

Clyde was not sure what Howie was trying to protect—the company's best interests or his own position of power. He suspected it was the latter. Howie's title of CEO these past few months had bestowed on him authority and decision-making power. It had affected what he did day to day.

The founders' conversation went on for several hours. Clyde

remained convinced that they had no choice but to give up control if they wanted to raise VC money. Howie acknowledged this as a possibility but refused to accept it outright, much less to use it as a strategy to attract VCs. He kept reiterating, "We want to run our company if at all possible." And he worried that if they told the VCs that they would give up control, it would be inevitable that they would have to give up control.

However, as it grew late and time to find a solution was clearly running short, Howie agreed that they should be open to the VCs' suggestions about changes in management. Howie concurred that they would "push for control but also be careful not to push too hard," and Clyde consented not to force decisions about their management roles until absolutely necessary.

꜀

After this meeting, it quickly became apparent that Howie and Clyde perceived each other's words as *empty promises*. Later that night, Clyde pulled me aside and whispered, "I am worried, very worried that Howie has not really come to understand the severity of the situation, and that in our next meeting with a VC he will still not convey a willingness to give up control." Clyde put it plainly, "Howie wants to be CEO, and he is unwilling to recognize the need to give this up."

The next morning, when Howie and I were alone, he also told me that he was not satisfied with where the conversation had ended. He worried, "Clyde is so willing to give up control that he is just going to offer it without any resistance."

꜀

For the next few days, Howie and Clyde said little to each other. With five days to go before they were scheduled to leave for California to meet with potential venture capitalists, Aaron and

Daniel decided that they had no choice but to intervene and try to restore respect between Howie and Clyde. They decided that they would together talk first with Clyde and then with Howie. They asked them one at a time to come into the conference room and to state the problem from their perspective.

From this exercise, they learned that Clyde's critical concern was that he had found a potential CEO candidate, Lawrence, and that Howie was not following up with him. Clyde believed that they needed to build up a team of professional managers and that they needed to be actively interviewing. He didn't trust Howie to find a replacement for himself. In his mind, the main problem was that Howie was "power hungry and does not want to step down as CEO."

When Howie was alone in the conference room and Aaron and Daniel asked him about Clyde, Howie's pent-up resentment quickly became apparent. Turning beet red, he blurted out, "He has no respect for others. He is not changeable. He has been like this since he joined the company. He annoys me. He is not a team player. He is a detriment to our company's success. Clyde does not listen. He is incompetent. He simply has no respect for me. This has gotten worse ever since Clyde decided I should not be CEO, but this has been going on all along." About the CEO candidate, Lawrence, Howie told Aaron and Daniel that Lawrence was not the right person for the job. Several times Howie repeated that while he recognized he might have to step down, before he did, he wanted to make sure they had found the right person to take his place.

After hearing both sides, Daniel and Aaron shared their own opinions. They both had had trouble with Clyde in the past for the same reasons Howie had outlined. However, recently they had found Clyde to be improving. As for Howie, they shared Clyde's concern that he wouldn't give up his position. They worried about Howie's desire to be in control, and they feared that in the future he would not be effective as the CEO. They thought

Howie was too opinionated and stubborn, which caused unnecessary friction.

To get Howie to step down, however, Aaron and Daniel realized that they first had to figure out an alternative role for him to play in the company. After giving the matter some thought, Aaron volunteered that Howie could take his position as chief technical officer. Daniel agreed that that might appeal to Howie. It was more likely that Howie would be able to hold on to the title of CTO even after the VCs brought in a new CEO.

Daniel and Aaron finally decided to get Howie and Clyde together in the conference room, letting first Howie and then Clyde state his case. They agreed that each would present his perspective, uninterrupted by the other.

Howie went first. Looking directly at Clyde, he said, "You don't respect me or what I am doing. You don't respond to my e-mails. You don't believe me, you second-guess me. You think I shouldn't be CEO; you think my position is invalid. You don't do what I ask or what is in the best interest of the company. Your attitude is not getting us anywhere. I cannot continue with your attitude. We are not working as a team."

When Howie finished, Clyde replied, "Whenever there is a problem, you won't address it. You run away from it; you make sarcastic remarks. If there is something to resolve, you won't say it and deal with it. You just think what you say should go because you are CEO. These things should be team decisions, not your decisions."

After each had had his turn to speak uninterrupted, a round of bickering and finger-pointing ensued. There was no exploration or engagement of the deeper issues, much less hope of resolution.

Finally, not knowing what else to do, Aaron said, "Look, I don't know what the solution to the problem is. You are a bunch of immature people who need to be friends and go on together."

Daniel added, "I am worried about us all. It is all of us

together: you, me, the four of us, those who work here, the friends and family who put money into this."

Aaron broke back in, "We need to be big enough to realize the greater good."

Seeking solutions rather than more accusations and blame, Daniel suggested they address specific issues, one at a time. Howie started by stating his doubts about Lawrence as a potential CEO candidate. Although Lawrence had an impressive record, he had no experience with college students, marketing, or the Internet. After voicing these reservations, Howie continued, "I left it with Lawrence that he would check out our website and we would look over his résumé." Clyde was surprised to learn that Howie had followed up with Lawrence at all.

This led them into a discussion about the bigger issue: replacing Howie as CEO. Aaron and Daniel tried to sell Howie on their new idea that he should become the CTO. Howie agreed to take on the role of CTO, but only after they had found a suitable person to replace him as CEO. For the time being, Howie made it clear he had no intention of stepping aside. Howie did admit that Versity needed an experienced CEO and that he needed to be open to finding that person. However, that acknowledgment changed nothing from Howie's perspective. He continued to believe that he was the best CEO for Versity, at least for the time being. And, indeed, no one had expressed to him anything to the contrary.

༃

Aaron, Daniel—and Clyde—avoided mentioning to Howie their growing concerns that he was not fit to be CEO. In doing so, they prevented the discomfort associated with confronting Howie about his unduly high regard for his own managerial capabilities. However, they also prevented Howie from learning that they believed Versity would be a better place with a new leader.

Howie had no idea that they believed he had major short-comings as their leader, let alone what those shortcomings were. All Howie knew was that they feared that to raise money he'd have to agree to step down. Without gaining an understanding of what his co-founders truly thought, Howie had no chance to address the weaknesses they perceived.

At the same time, because his co-founders were *patching* over his desire to remain CEO by offering him the role of CTO, it was difficult for Howie to keep complaining. For Howie to challenge the unsatisfactory nature of such a patch would have required confronting his co-founders, who, he realized, believed that they had made a valiant effort to find him this alternative role.

Patching has an end result similar to that of suppressing: someone feels forced to silence, but the underlying issue remains. The key difference is that with patching, the solution, while obviously superficial, still suggests that the silencer cared enough to try to accommodate. And, because the silencer has modified his own behavior, he feels better about himself and how he's treated the other person. However, to confront a patch is all the more difficult for this very reason—because the silencer believes he's already made an effort to address the difference.

⌇

Once Howie finally expressed his willingness to accept the patch and take on the role of CTO, Clyde felt more confident that Howie would signal that willingness when they met with poten-tial VCs. Howie, however, still did not feel Clyde had made com-parable concessions. When asked about his level of comfort with Clyde at this point, Howie first responded to Aaron and Daniel, saying, "Clyde needs to understand the importance of being a team player." Next, he turned to Clyde, looked straight at him, and said, "We need to work as a team, and you don't."

In response to this personal attack, Clyde asked for examples. Eventually Clyde assented, "I agree I can be a stubborn bastard, but that is who I am." He contended that this was just how he operated. "I make a decision and then find so much to support it, I cannot see the other side." Realizing time was fleeting, however, Clyde agreed to try to act differently. Most of all he did not want to do anything that might interfere with Versity's ability to raise the money that they so desperately needed.

By agreeing, Clyde made it seem to those involved that they had succeeded in telling him something he needed to hear. But actually, Clyde remained unconvinced that it was necessary or valuable for him to change. Rather, he was *making an empty promise.*

Once again, Howie and Clyde were choosing to address the current crisis at the expense of their longer-term relationship. Neither had had the courage or the communication skills to air their deeper concerns in a way that the other could hear and understand. Nor had either of them taken the responsibility to try to understand the other's point of view or question what was at the source of their issues. Rather, confronting looming deadlines, they didn't think they had time to "waste" dealing with their issues. Yet, by not effectively discussing their differences, they further reinforced a pattern of not confronting these differences—thus making effectively expressing their differences all the more unlikely in the future. What made this moment especially poignant, however, was that they both truly believed that they were doing the right thing, the reasonable thing, the mature thing, by letting their issues go and getting on with preparations for their trip to California.

⟋⟍

While in California, Howie and Clyde spent the whole time running from one appointment to the next. At one point, they were rushing from a meeting in San Francisco to one forty-five minutes down the peninsula in Palo Alto. They were halfway there when they realized that the valet had given them the wrong car. It was the same type of car that they had rented, so they didn't notice at first. But when they went to change the radio station, they realized it was set to a station to which they never listened. As they looked around, they suddenly realized that this was not their car. Now they had to speed back into the city, switch cars, and still make it to their next appointment on time. For most, this would have been an impossible feat. For Howie and Clyde, it was just another hurdle in the race to get Versity off and running.

ঔ

By all accounts, their trip to California was a success. A number of venture capital firms in Silicon Valley showed interest.

A partner at Sigma Partners liked what he heard when he met with Howie and Clyde. He noted to me later, "I found it all quite enticing. They are good guys. I think very highly of them. They are hardworking. They have a great culture. They are dedicated and committed."

An associate at Venrock Associates, Gordon, recalled for me in a personal conversation, "My plate is full and I didn't want to like them when they came. But I was very impressed with them as people, their enthusiasm and commitment. I was also impressed by their plan, how well they have done already, how well they know their market, and how well they have thought through their business. They are young, but they are very impressive. They have just gone out and done it, and it seems to be catching on."

What particularly struck Gordon was how seamlessly Howie and Clyde worked together. "It was most impressive how they tag-teamed the various slides they used in the presentation. They both seemed perfectly in synch with the other, and the transitions were so natural we hardly noticed." Gordon interpreted this as an indication of their strength as a team. Indeed, in the face of the shared goal of impressing the VCs, Howie and Clyde had managed to cover up their differences so successfully that the VCs had come to see their relationship as a selling point of the deal.

This is noteworthy not just because of the image Howie and Clyde were able to convey but because of the value attached to this image and the resources that are often associated with it. Indeed, there is a prevalent tendency in our society to associate value with teamwork and to use consensus as an indicator of teamwork. We tend to favor a team of people who express agreement over one in which members bicker over ideas. And, indeed, there are often rewards for acting in this more harmonious way—in this case, Howie and Clyde interested Venrock in investing as a result. Yet when team members don't express their differences, they miss out on the potential to learn from those differences and to produce better-quality output as a result.[3]

༄

When one of the partners at Venrock learned that his firm was interested in funding a deal with Versity but first wanted to try to find a new CEO, he recommended Peter. Peter had been his classmate at Harvard Business School, and the two had recently reconnected at their twentieth reunion. Another one of their classmates was Meg Whitman, the well-publicized CEO of eBay, the online auction company. Peter had shown great fascination with Meg's story and with the burgeoning possibilities of the Internet. Knowing Peter was looking for a new job, the Venrock partner suspected that he might just be interested in an opportunity to work with a dot-com that appeared so well poised for success.

CHAPTER SEVEN

The Founders and the New CEO Mask Their Differences

WHEN PETER first heard about Versity in July 1999, he was intrigued. He immediately saw many similarities to the types of challenges he faced at his previous firm, a large real estate conglomerate. Both companies were disparate organizations with representatives all over the country. Peter drew comparisons between the campus managers and his property managers. As president of his former company, Peter thought of himself as a coach and a mentor to teams operating in twenty-six markets. He had focused on creating a culture that fostered experimentation, risk taking, learning from mistakes, and empowerment. These were the very qualities he felt Versity needed to realize its potential as a leader in the college market.

A tall, soft-spoken, balding man, Peter spent the first Saturday in August at Versity, which happened to coincide with Versity's first-ever campus operations manager (COM) training. He observed the training, listening to the founders speak about their company's history, its progress to date, and its goals. A great believer in empowerment, Peter appreciated the way Howie appealed to the campus managers: "We are ready to go to ninety schools, and we need your help." Howie explained that what made Versity distinctive was knowing what students want, and that they as the campus managers knew best what the students at their schools wanted. He told them, "Each one of you in this room represents a campus, and each one of you can help us be a success on your campus."

Peter also heard the enthusiasm with which Daniel spoke about the products Versity was offering. One was a service Versity provided to remind students when they had exams or papers due. Daniel told one of his favorite stories, about visiting a school in Iowa. "I was there passing out fliers in one of the dorms. I went into one of the rooms and handed a flier to some kid still in bed. When the kid realized that I was from Versity, he sat up in bed and screamed, 'You saved me! You saved me! Last week I had a paper due worth 35 percent of my grade. I forgot. But you sent me an e-mail and saved me!'" Daniel laughed. "This kid was so excited, he let me plaster his entire room with Versity stickers."

After these initial introductions, COM training continued all day. The founders and Peter ducked out at lunch.

Throughout the day, Peter kept asking himself, "Who are the people I would work with? Are they good, committed, passionate people? Together, can we make whatever ends up being necessary happen?" What he had read about Versity all looked reasonable to him. He thought that the idea of aggregating all the "mom and pop" notes businesses was a good idea and that Versity had "a product that will wipe out the competition." His more pressing question had to do with the founders' passion for what they did. Were they truly committed to this enterprise?

Peter found himself answering "a resounding yes." He liked the founders and thought he would be able to work well with them. At the end of the day, he told them, "You guys are unique and wonderful. You have a passion. I will tell Venrock I will do this. I have been offered many opportunities, and I have done a lot more research, but on this I just have a gut feel."

He made clear to them that he was not interested in the job

for the financial rewards. He told them, "I have enough money. I never need to work again. This is about finding a passion, not about the work for the money." Indeed, Peter was thrilled with this opportunity. The learning curve excited him. "We will do this together, and we will collectively make mistakes. Together in one space, we will have a lot of energy."

Peter told me about his decision: "I am interested because the idea makes sense. I have great admiration for the founders and what they have already accomplished. Together we can build a great company and have fun while we are doing it." Peter was delighted to find a start-up in which he and the founders had such complementary skills. The founders had deep knowledge of the college market and the technology involved, yet relatively little business experience. Peter determined what they needed most was mentoring, which he believed was one of his greatest strengths.

After Peter left, the founders debriefed. They reviewed what they knew about Peter. He had expanded a real estate company nationally and widened its focus to include not just constructing apartments but also servicing the residents as consumers. As the company's founder, president, and board member, Peter had led the initial public offering and later merged the company to form a combined entity of approximately two thousand employees with a market cap of $4 billion and annual revenues of $500 million.

What amazed them was that Peter had done all of this in his forty-three years and yet he came across as so understated and agreeable. They found him smart, funny, even playful. What's more, he seemed to want to work with them, rather than replace them. They were excited and relieved that he said he wanted to be their coach and mentor, not their boss. They did wonder about his sincerity, and only hoped he meant what he had said.

᠅

The partners back at Venrock were delighted that Peter liked Versity so much. His enthusiasm solidified their own interest in funding the company. As Gordon, the associate at Venrock, put it, "I have never seen Peter in action, but he did run a $4 billion company, and there are just not that many people like that around." He called Peter "a gentleman, smart, and enthusiastic. He is not a slick salesman. There is no asshole component in him. He is sincere."

Kevin O'Connor, DoubleClick's CEO, had continued to be an informal mentor to the founders and had ultimately been a major investor in their first round of fundraising. When Kevin met with Peter, he gave Peter a thumbs-up. After meeting Peter, Kevin told me that he had been hoping they would find someone to lead Versity who was "smart, likes to win, and is willing to roll up his sleeves and get his hands dirty." Peter seemed to fit these qualifications. Kevin told the founders, "He is fired up, he is smart. I like him, Harvard is a great school, he has done start-ups. Hire him."

꒜

At Versity's headquarters, everyone was getting ready for the fall semester. They were expanding to nearly ninety schools. As part of this major launch, Jill, recently hired to head up public relations, organized an e-mail campaign to politely inform faculty that some students in their classes would serve as Versity note-takers. When professors learned that their students would be posting lecture notes on the Web, they reacted with fury. Immediately, Versity received thirty "angry" responses to the letter. There was surprise and concern in the office. No one had anticipated such a hostile reaction.

Versity's lawyers had been busy working on the details of the funding deal with the venture capitalists. It had been decided that Venrock would be the lead VC and that Sigma would be a co-investor, which meant Venrock would be in charge but Sigma would also invest several million dollars and receive a seat on the board of directors. The situation with the faculty, however, forced the lawyers to temporarily redirect their attention toward these potential lawsuits.

The founders had thought they were in the clear. Before starting Versity, they had looked into the legality of a notetaking enterprise. They had found that in 1996, professors at the University of Florida had tried to sue a notetaking service, but the federal court of Florida had filed in favor of the notetaking service. However, as Versity's lawyers now looked further into that case, they found that the Florida lawsuit had some loopholes. Although the notetakers had won, it was hard to say whether it was a true victory. Worse, the lawyers discovered another case in California that in 1969 had ruled in favor of the university over the notetaking business. In response, the lawyers advised the founders that posting notes, according to legal precedent, was an infringement of intellectual property rights and a violation of copyright law. The lawyers recommended that Versity immediately remove from their website notes for any class whose professor had asked them to do so. The founders obliged.

The deal with Venrock and Sigma was scheduled to close on September 9, 1999. As luck would have it, that same morning a story ran on the front page of *The New York Times*: "Free College Notes on Web: Aid to Learning or Laziness." The article was about one of their competitors, StudentU, and contained many quotes from distressed professors. Although the founders were able to reassure themselves and the VCs that Versity was a much stronger company than StudentU, they worried about the online notes business being so poorly positioned in the media.

Peter was in New York City with Clyde, meeting with some potential business partners, when he saw the article. He told me over the phone, "I've been in business long enough to appreciate the significance of front-page coverage in *The New York Times*.

This is just the tip of the iceberg." Peter believed that the article would have severe ramifications for the nascent online notes industry and for Versity.

ॐ

As it turned out, what held up the deal with Venrock and Sigma was not the legal issues with outraged professors or the *New York Times* piece. The big issue was Peter's employment contract. Clyde, who had never negotiated an employment contract before, was responsible for reaching an agreement with Peter. Without Peter, both of them knew full well, there would be no funding from Venrock. Peter, aware that he was in an extremely powerful negotiating position, tried to take full advantage of it.

Peter's hardball negotiation left the founders wondering about him, the role he would play in their company, and the potential relationship that they would have with him.

ॐ

Howie and Clyde's confidence in each other had been in jeopardy ever since Clyde had silenced himself in response to their first dispute over managing. They were able to stave off the more recent issue over leadership by *glossing over* their issues. Now, with new management coming in and change at all levels of the company occurring, their old tensions were resurfacing.

Howie resorted to sending Clyde an e-mail.[1] Clyde quickly responded, using bold font to intersperse his reactions into Howie's message.

> HOWIE: I find your behavior with Peter a bit problematic. It seems like you're trying to position yourself better with new management and investors.
> **CLYDE: Frankly, I have been positioning myself well with**

Peter and our new investors because I want to learn from them and make sure that I remain in the loop with what is going on. However, I do not do it at the expense of you or anyone else.

HOWIE: After all this, you and Peter have been honeymooning while quite frankly, I am back here holding the [expletive] company together. I'm handling issues with PR, technology, I'm still having to do much of CoreTex myself, in addition to everything else. . . . The changes that are going on are difficult enough, without your seemingly underhanded attempt to get on Peter's "good" side, at my expense.

CLYDE: I consistently brag about you to Peter and everyone else I talk to because, in my view, you created this company. Although we do occasionally have our differences (always over sorts of control issues), the fact remains that you are the only other person in this company that I have complete faith in. There is no way I could be where I am right now without you and no way you could be where you are without me. The best thing about us is our skills are not "competitive," and I would never feel the need to get ahead at your expense. I hope you believe me on that.

HOWIE: All I know is I'm working myself to death here. (I'm . . . having dizzy spells and it scares me) trying to put out fire after fire, and you're positioning me poorly with Peter as a result. It's not appreciated.

CLYDE: I appreciate your hard work just like I hope you appreciate mine. Anything I can do to help, let me know, and do not blame me for positioning you poorly. You can position yourself with him, and I think the problem is that you are resisting giving him a lot of control. You could relieve a lot of stress from yourself if you talked to him more. . . . I appreciate your candidness and honesty, and I hope we can work through this stuff. I do not want you to feel this way, and I will make whatever effort I can to make you feel more comfortable. You and I need to be careful to not let these things escalate, and you handled this very professionally to stop the spiraling effect.

When Howie received Clyde's response, he said and did nothing. Howie did not believe that Clyde actually cared to know what he could do to help or how he could make Howie feel more comfortable. Howie suspected that Clyde was again *making empty promises.* He interpreted Clyde's response in this e-mail as nothing more than fancy footwork, believing that Clyde had no interest in helping him. Reflecting on earlier incidents, Howie had come to believe that Clyde had a pattern of indicating he would do something when he was merely saying so to avoid confrontation and had no real intent of changing anything. Howie had reached the point where he was skeptical about whatever Clyde said (and did not say) in this kind of situation.

౿

On September 14, 1999, the funding deal with Venrock as the lead venture capitalist was signed. Versity had raised $11.2 million on top of a $15 million premoney valuation, surpassing the founders' wildest dreams.

౿

Peter came back to Michigan as the new CEO, meeting with different people and trying to make sense of the company he had agreed to lead. He focused on identifying the problems he saw at Versity so that he could begin to address them.

Peter was focusing entirely on the big picture, not the details. At one point, when he was busy talking about the "C-O-Ms,"

Howie interrupted him in frustration, as if he had already corrected him a hundred times: "Peter, they are '*COMs.*'" Later in the day, despite Howie's prods, Peter was still talking about the "C-O-Ms," not the "COMs."

At a different point in the day, Aaron went running after Clyde, attempting to conk him with a big piece of Styrofoam. As he chased Clyde, he charged right past Peter. Like a kid about to do something his father would not approve of, Aaron stopped, looked first at Peter, then at Clyde, thought for a second, then banged Clyde over the head. It was a key moment. Without saying a word, Aaron made it clear: "I am not going to act differently just because you, Peter, are around." Peter did not respond at first. Then he broke out in laughter, as if he thought it was just as funny as they did. Although Peter first impressed the founders as a smooth and polished corporate businessman, he was quickly revealing a playful spirit. Indeed, he later remarked to me, "I worry you might think I am still twenty-two, or want to be twenty-two."

Peter was trying hard to relate to the founders on the superficial issues of how they interacted—in terms of the games they played and the fun they had. However, when it came to the future direction of the company, Peter focused on what he perceived to be the areas of greatest concern—the lack of infrastructure and their technology shortcomings. Getting caught up in the semantics over details such as whether they were "C-O-Ms" or "COMs" simply was not important to him.

৵

As Peter's familiarity with Versity grew, he wavered back and forth about the opportunities that lay ahead. At some moments, Peter's enthusiasm entirely dwarfed his concerns. He gloated about how the notes industry was so fragmented that Versity did not have a single big competitor. He was also coming to see a real advantage of having a distribution network of students on campuses across the country. Many people were already approaching him to partner so they could have access to Versity's local distribution network. He noted, "We are going to be able to use our network for multiple profit-making enterprises."

At other moments, however, Peter's enthusiasm waned. He had learned that Snowball, another dot-com pursuing the college market, had allotted $6 to $8 million for advertising alone. He explained to me, "I am worried, worried about the competitors and worried that [the founders] don't realize that they need to keep fighting and they have a long way to go."

Peter further considered the technical glitches with their website deeply problematic, lamenting to me, "My site stinks. We are out telling everyone it is a learning center, and yet our page is a mess and things that should be up are not." The day the company website crashed twelve times disturbed Peter profoundly. Even though Aaron stayed up all night and finally stabilized the site, Peter felt they needed more technical expertise on board, and they needed it quickly.

Following the *New York Times* article, the National Association of College and University Attorneys met to discuss the legality of online notetaking and decided it was not an actionable item. The student is paying to be in the class, they reasoned, and a student's interpretation of a faculty's lecture is not the intellectual property of that faculty. As long as students were posting their own interpretations, it appeared to be okay from a legal standpoint. Peter felt great relief knowing that his business was legal.

Then, only days later, Princeton University made using online notes against its honor code. Peter suddenly recognized "the real potential downfall of our business." Up until this point, what he and the VCs had worried about were legal and intellectual property issues. They had underestimated the power of the universities to make their own rules. Peter drew a parallel to his experience in the real estate industry: "It is like forgetting about the neighbors and the zoning issues. These are real issues that can stop you and leave you with no way to appeal." He kept repeating to me that he and the VCs had never realized this threat to their business. When Peter discussed the news with Gordon, the Venrock associate working on the deal, they agreed that Princeton's actions signaled the potential downfall of Versity's core business model. Gordon suggested that they needed an alternative plan, and together they started to brainstorm. They concluded that although notes might not be a viable business plan, there were other types of businesses in the online education market that might still be feasible.

The first month on the job proved quite stressful. The more Peter learned about the challenges facing Versity—both externally and internally—the more he felt he needed help. He wanted to hire people who could help fix their technical problems, but he also wanted an experienced technical manager who would be able to translate the issues into a form Peter could understand and therefore better assess. Peter had also discovered that Versity had no financial plan, no health plan, and nothing in place that resembled infrastructure. He wanted to hire people to help handle these shortcomings, people who could be fully dedicated to the internal, day-to-day operations so he could focus on all the external problems.

In discussions with the founders, Peter initially tried to discuss the problems he saw at Versity, but the founders got defensive. Peter confided in me, "When I tell [the founders] about problems, they get upset. I am working on being more political in how I tell things to the guys. I do not want to upset them, but at the same time I am very concerned that things are not working, and we need to get them fixed, immediately." The Peter who confided in me bore little resemblance to the Peter the founders were getting to know. When Peter talked to me, he was often distressed, impatient, sometimes even disgusted. He described how terrible the website was, how everything was messed up, and how many issues they had with public relations. With the founders, however, in an effort to maintain their confidence and respect, he hid his true thoughts and feelings. He said nothing about what he believed needed to be done internally, nor did he say anything about all the external problems, including the possibility that Versity might need to shift its business model.

As much as Peter worried about creating an organizational infrastructure, fixing the technical problems, and addressing their external crises, he also wanted to establish a good working relationship with the founders. Believing that too much criticism of the company at this early stage might send their relationship down a negative path—sidetracking them from achieving their primary goal of creating the most successful company possible—Peter only communicated a sense of urgency to hire and fill what he referred to as all the "open slots."[2] He said he was looking for a CFO, a vice president (VP) of business development, a VP of marketing, a VP of engineering, someone to do recruiting and training, and an executive assistant. He asserted that Versity needed these people to help grow the company to the next level, and that Versity needed them quickly. The founders were well aware of Peter's eagerness to hire all these new people, but they never understood the reason behind the urgency.

By not clarifying the problems that he believed needed to be addressed for the company to be able to grow successfully, what Peter did not recognize was that he was making it harder for the founders to make sense of the changes he had in mind. And lacking understanding of his perspective, the founders would later be resistant to changes he thought were obviously critical.

Moreover, by saying little about his feelings and not explaining his actions, Peter helped set in motion a norm of silencing between himself and the founders. And, because Peter was the CEO, his silencing had an effect far beyond each of his individual relationships. When a senior manager like Peter silences himself or others, they sow the seeds of an organizational culture of silencing.[3] And, as I discussed in Chapter 2, a culture of silencing has a profound impact on how members of the organization act when experiencing a difference in thought or feeling with another.

ॐ

During the month between the closing of the funding deal and the move to California—scheduled for October 15, 1999—Peter made a weekly overnight trip to Michigan. Otherwise he was in California preparing for the company's arrival, searching desperately for office space and more experienced people to help him grow the company.

Hal was the first potential hire that Peter introduced to the founders. Peter described to the founders some of the famous ad campaigns that Hal, a longtime friend, had written and directed for such clients as Taco Bell and Pepsi. He also told them how Hal had headed up creative design at the well-regarded marketing firms of Saatchi & Saatchi and Bozell Worldwide.

Hal visited the Michigan office. He seemed much older than Peter, in demeanor if not in age. Like a college marketing professor giving an impromptu lecture, Hal talked on about his philosophy of branding by knowing your customer. The founders, hungry for whatever they could learn about marketing, listened eagerly as he shared his wisdom. After Hal's visit, no one objected to his potential involvement with the company.

Hal, too, was excited. As he summed up his visit, "My mind is running wild. I like the idea and the market. There is a huge market and so much we can do." However, Hal was reluctant to commit to a full-time job. He agreed, instead, to be a consultant and the short-term acting head of marketing. Part of his agreement was that he would help find and hire a longer-term vice president of marketing.

Next Peter introduced the founders to Kristin, a candidate for vice president of business development. Kristin, who had an MBA degree from Harvard and had been a captain in the Marine Corps, came across as tough, aggressive, and career oriented. The founders took Kristin to lunch. At one point, they started asking what she would do if a bucket of water were to be poured on her head. Although this woman had had an answer for everything, there now was a long pause, and then she just said sternly, "I certainly hope this would not happen before a meeting." As I listened to this conversation, I could not help but wonder if she realized this sort of thing happened all the time at Versity, though usually late at night.

Daniel, in debriefing with the other founders after Kristin left, summed up their shared opinion: "She is not the right person. She has no Internet experience, and, worse than that, she does not fit our culture." Clyde called Peter to relay the founders' sentiment. He told Peter, "The reason we brought you in is because you are someone we want to learn from. She is not." To their delight, Peter dropped her as a possible hire.

Peter also found a CFO candidate, whom Clyde described as "totally *not* Internet savvy." Clyde noted, "He does not even have a computer at home, and he doesn't know how to use e-mail." When Peter tried to make the case that their CFO did not need to be technically competent, Clyde objected, "He needs to at least be able to communicate by e-mail." They agreed not to hire him.

The founders felt good that Peter was listening to their opinions, though they worried about how many people they could veto before it became a problem.

Their lawyer recommended Jim, also for the CFO position. Jim was Peter's age, lived in California, and seemed to Peter to be well qualified for the job. He had previously been the CFO or controller for four companies and had even been promoted to president at one of them. He also had a great deal of experience in high-tech industries and start-ups. Jim's visit to Michigan, however, left the founders lukewarm. Clyde cautioned that three of Jim's past companies had failed. He also worried whether Jim was assertive enough.

The founders did not dislike Jim, but they were not impressed by him. They expressed their reactions to Peter. Anxious to fill the position of CFO, Peter placed great weight on Jim's references. One woman on the board of directors of Jim's previous employer assured Peter that Jim was smart, handled complexity well, and always kept the board abreast not just of the numbers but of what was really happening. "There are no skeletons in the closet," she noted. Peter offered Jim the job. And Jim, buying into Peter's enthusiasm, accepted it.

For the position of vice president of product development, Gordon, the Venrock associate, referred Peter to Dave. Dave had been working for a medical software company since graduating from Stanford Business School seven years earlier. The CEO of Dave's company had wanted to win the prestigious Malcolm Baldrige National Quality Award, given to companies that maintain the highest level of quality in the country. Dave's role was to go around to different groups within the eleven-hundred-person organization, listen to them, and work together to fix their problems. His job changed every quarter, helping him to learn every dimension of the business. In three years, he led the company to implement a world-class management system that won the Malcolm Baldridge Award. Then Dave went on within the company to work in customer support and regulatory affairs. Peter thought Dave's background made him the perfect person to help create order out of all the chaos at Versity. Peter believed that his own greatest weakness was running the internal operations of the company, and he thought Dave's skills would nicely complement his own.

To the founders, Dave was "intelligent, but boring." They

felt they could work with him, but they just did not like him. The founders, however, felt they had no choice but to agree to hiring Dave. They recognized they could not veto everyone.

When Peter offered Dave the job of VP of product development, he accepted. Dave told me, "My last job was not much fun. This job seems like it will be great fun." According to his employment contract, Dave was in charge of product development, but Peter already had other plans for him. The two of them had discussed Dave taking on the role of COO, in charge of all internal matters. Although Peter would have liked to hire Dave into that position immediately, he decided that, given the founders' reluctance, he would wait until Dave first had a chance to prove himself. Nothing about Dave's becoming COO was ever mentioned to the founders.

Peter's *patch* regarding Dave's role—making him vice president of product development instead of COO—resembled Clyde, Aaron, and Daniel's earlier attempt to ease Howie out of the role of CEO, offering him the title of CTO instead. By not discussing the deeper issues with the founders, Peter never came to understand their objection to Dave, nor did they understand the reasons behind Peter's strong support for Dave. Better understanding on both sides would likely have led to a decision with mutual consent and more respect—whether the decision was to make Dave COO or not to hire him at all.

Beyond these key hires, the partner at Venrock working with Versity recommended that Peter contact Sharon for the position of vice president of human resources. Sharon had been supporting a group of seven thousand employees at Seagate Technology. Peter interviewed and hired her before the founders ever had a chance to meet her.

At this point, Peter had successfully hired three key members of his management team—CFO, VP of product development, and VP of human resources. In Silicon Valley during this period of time, there was a shortage of managerial talent, not money, and Peter was thrilled to have found such qualified people to join him so quickly.

The founders were not sure what to make of all the hiring. They still were unaware of all the problems Peter perceived. As Aaron said to me, "To his credit, Peter is enthusiastic about the company and is bringing in older people who do have more experience. I like that Peter is selling them on the company. I like that Peter sees the great opportunity here and is creating interest for others. But I am not sure why these people or where all of this is leading." The others agreed. They liked Peter's enthusiasm but wondered why he felt so much pressure to bring in people who to them did not seem well qualified for their positions.

Peter's choices raised questions in the founders' minds about his ability to understand and lead this type of company. As Daniel explained to me, "At first I felt very positive about Peter. He had interesting experience, and I liked his management philosophy. But now I am not sure. I think he is a good guy. I just hope he is the right guy. I think he is. I don't expect him to ruin the company. I think we have a lot to gain from him. But I am worried about how he has been acting. I am worried about all these new hires. On the other hand, we have built the company this far, and having some professionals take the reins and teach us is a real opportunity. So part of me is excited about learning from others who know more. I just hope these are the right people."

The founders said nothing more to Peter about the people whom he had chosen. Just as Peter purposefully silenced his criticism of the company, the founders carefully did not verbalize their criticism of his hires.

Peter had heard the founders' initial questions about some of the people he had hired, but then they said nothing more. He had expected that it would be difficult for the founders to give up control. Over time, though, he assumed that their issues would naturally disappear. And that was what appeared to have happened. Peter had no reason to suspect that the founders had silenced themselves and were harboring any resentment for what had occurred. Rather, he just assumed that they had come to appreciate that he knew what he was doing.

For Peter, the looming crisis was the state of the company and what had to be done to get it into shape. His new hires were a relief, as he hoped they would help address his growing concerns about the internal workings of the company. Still, he said nothing to the founders about his worries, hoping that the people he had hired would make the problems disappear.

Everyone was engaging in *silencing themselves,* but on very different issues, with different rationales. Unlike Howie and Clyde, who often spoke to each other about their differences but in destructive ways—personally attacking and threatening each other and failing to listen and respond to each other—the founders and professional managers were not talking to one another about their differences. Not talking, however, is no better. They too were setting in motion an interpersonal climate characterized by distrust, lack of respect, and norms of silence.

჻

The management team now consisted of the newly hired managers—Peter (CEO), Jim (CFO), Dave (VP of product development), Sharon (VP of HR), Hal (the consultant and acting head of marketing), and a handful of people from the Michigan office, including the founders as well as some older hires like Jill (public relations), Mark (campus operations), and Rob (product development).

Howie had officially become the chief technology officer (CTO), and since Peter had had no success in hiring a vice president of engineering, Howie headed up the technical group. Aaron had become just one of the engineers in that group. Dave took over product development, and Daniel reported to him. Clyde was put in charge of business development until a vice president of business development could be hired.

The venture capitalists made it clear to the new professional managers that they should keep the founders actively involved. As one of them put it clearly to Peter, "The founders need to be kept in the inner circle. They are key people. They are the talent and passion behind this organization. They care more than anyone else. They hold a lot of equity, and they want the company to do well." The VC added, "We invested because of the founders, and we want to make sure to keep them involved." Peter had no problem with this. He fully agreed that the founders were central to the business.

ᢒ

When the group from Michigan arrived in California in the middle of October, Peter had already found office space to rent. However, nothing was set up—not the phones, not the network for the computers. Before much else could be accomplished, the engineers were needed to help hook everything up. The founders were surprised and disappointed. Why, they wondered, had Peter disrupted everyone's work and moved them across the country before the office was ready? But there was so much to be done that they had little time to wonder.

Just before they left Michigan, the website had developed some new technical glitches, and it kept crashing. However, once in California, instead of being able to concentrate on the problems with their website, the engineers found themselves stuck setting up the new office. Peter recognized this distraction and knew that the engineers were working as hard as they could. Still, he could not help but worry about all the technical problems with the site and whether they could handle them all internally.

Peter had searched hard to find a vice president of engineering. But he had not yet found someone to hire. He worried greatly that neither he nor any of his senior hires truly understood the technical aspects of their business. If only he could find a highly skilled manager to head the technical operations, he reasoned, it would not matter that all his new hires lacked technical knowledge. According to Peter, a good vice president of engineering not only would effectively manage the technical aspects of their business but could serve as a translator to help the rest of the management team make more informed decisions. Having not yet hired this person, it was difficult for Peter even to assess the magnitude of their technical problems.

༄

Within a week of their arrival in California, Versity's newly formed board of directors convened for the first time. Peter was chairman of the board. He, the Venrock partner, the Sigma partner, and Howie all had voting rights. The other three founders, several other investors, and the company lawyer had nonvoting observer rights.

Early in the board meeting, Peter mentioned all the technical problems that they were having. The venture capitalists immediately decided that outside help was essential and started suggesting who could provide the necessary technical support. Howie wanted to back up and first explain what was going on with the website and what he was planning to do about it. He believed that their technical problems were on the verge of being solved and that hiring technical consultants would be a waste of time and money, especially before they solved the immediate crisis and had time to assess their needs. But the other board members thought that there was no time to spare, and the conversation quickly degenerated into a competition among the VCs as to who could find someone to provide Versity better help faster. Howie kept trying to get them to stop attempting to outdo each other and start focusing on the problem, but no one was listening to him.

⟜

After the meeting, Howie remained confused about the logic behind hiring technical consultants. As Dave explained it to me, "Howie is asking the wrong question. He is asking whether it is the right thing to do to hire consultants. The board does not care whether or not it is the right thing to do. The board wants it done. They have the money, and they are willing to spend it to find out whether or not it is the right thing to do. They would rather find out they are wrong but know they have tried than have a shadow of doubt that they could have done it differently." Dave continued, "The board would rather spend a lot of money and make it big, with the risk of failure, than spend less money and have less probability of making it big." From the venture capitalists' perspective, time, not money, was the precious commodity. They wanted to invest whatever it would take, so they would know as soon as possible whether the company had the potential to succeed.

By subtly suppressing Howie in the meeting, the board members had avoided having to consider Howie's ideas, ideas they perceived they had no time or need to consider. This indeed may have been the most desirable approach for them in this circumstance. When time pressure is great and a course of action is clear to those in power, the benefits of hearing additional opinions or perspectives may not outweigh the costs.

There are still costs, however, that should not be overlooked but rather must be addressed in due course. Just because a disagreement has been suppressed does not mean that so, too, has the resistance. People's convictions are seldom changed by forced compliance. Privately, Howie wondered more than ever about the decision to bring in professional managers who lacked a technical background. And although addressing Howie's issues in the meeting might well have been inappropriate, these issues needed to be addressed at some point before it was too late and they grew into even larger issues.

Peter and Howie's relationship would have benefited greatly if after the meeting one had sought the other out to discuss what had occurred. Peter could have taken the initiative to explain to Howie why the board had felt it necessary to move on despite Howie's dissent. Or Howie might have put a set of genuine questions to Peter about what had happened—expressing curiosity and seeking insight, as opposed to just defending his own actions or saying nothing.

و٭

Howie did not disagree that there was a problem with the website. He told me, "Tech right now is the biggest letdown in the company. Every marketing dollar is wasted if we are trying to get people to visit the site and the site does not work, and every product development dollar is wasted if the site does not work." He described the immense pressure he felt. "The tech team is ridiculously burnt out. They have been taken through the wringer and back. There has been one emergency after the next for the past six months. I have been working seven days a week to try to fix things. We need help. The problems are over our head."

To Howie, the question, however, was how best to address their problems, and in what sequence. The site crashes had become much worse in the previous week because the engineers had had to spend so much time setting up the office. Howie's top priority was to stabilize the site. Until they solved that problem, Versity would continue to lose users. Howie felt that it was essential to take time to get that problem under control first, before looking into whether to hire consultants, and if so, whom to hire. Howie recognized that consultants could be necessary for helping to create longer-term site reliability, but he felt strongly that this should not be the immediate focus of attention.

Howie shared all of these thoughts with me, but with no one else.

※

Feeling defeated after the meeting, Howie agreed to hire consultants. When he learned that it would take six weeks and cost $250,000, he was all the more distressed. Plus, the consultants wanted to switch the language in which the site was programmed, from Cold Fusion to Java. Howie explained to me, "The two are very different languages, and while Java may be better longer term, no one in our company knows Java. We will all need to get retrained. There is a steep learning curve." Howie stated his biggest worry: "We will end up with a problematic architecture and no one to support it."

※

Frustrated that he could not get Peter to listen to his perspective, Howie felt that he no longer had a voice in the important decisions of the company, even when he was the only one with relevant expertise. "Peter just does not understand what is going on with tech. All he knows is when he wants something and it is not working," Howie griped. In response, Howie basically gave up trying to be heard. This behavior, however, only further substantiated Peter's impression of Howie—that Howie lacked judgment and maturity and therefore was unsuitable to help in the ways Peter felt Versity so desperately needed help. They still hadn't found a vice president of engineering, but Peter had no hope that Howie could temporarily play this role.

Howie and Peter kept feeding each other's suspicions,

becoming less and less trusting and respectful of the other and increasingly self-protective in the process. The more Peter distanced himself from Howie, the more convinced Howie was that Peter was not willing to listen to the technical issues that were salient to run a technical business, and so the less he tried to communicate them. However, the more Howie silenced himself in the face of Peter's apparent rejection, the less Howie provided the necessary information. And the more Howie failed to provide the necessary information, the more Peter doubted Howie's ability and willingness to serve the critical role of translator of technical issues. In turn, Peter felt an even greater need to hire a vice president of engineering who could play this role.

Here we see a powerful example of how Peter's desire for the company to move as fast as possible with its technological development actually caused even more pressure to go fast. Peter's perception that he didn't have time to hear Howie out in the board meeting nor after it caused Howie to become all the less effective at the job and made the pressure to find a vice president of engineering all the more urgent. The need for speed in dealing with the technical issues ended up creating an even more pressing need for speed.

Peter and Howie were unknowingly caught up in the silent spiral, and their need for speed was only making it all the worse. Neither was talking about his concerns or figuring out how to work together most effectively. This was particularly unfortunate, given that they each brought important skills that had the potential to help guide them through this tough period. If done with a genuine desire to enhance each other's understanding— as opposed to initiating a bickering match of escalating confrontation—discussing these issues openly might well have enabled Howie and Peter to find a way to work together effectively and to cope with their problems despite not yet having found a vice president of engineering.

Howie may have lacked the experience and polish of the

senior, professional vice president of engineering that Peter would have liked to hire, but Howie was a bright, competent technical whiz kid. If encouraged and guided, Howie could most certainly have provided at least some of the information the management team so desperately needed. And, given the chance to perform, Howie would likely have gained Peter's respect. As Peter gained respect and started to listen to Howie, Howie would likely have become more receptive to his views. Howie, in turn, feeling that his perspective was being heard, would likely have gained more respect for Peter.

Having achieved greater respect for each other, they would then have been better able to benefit from each other's strengths—together figuring out how Howie could best play the desperately needed role of technical translator for a set of technically inexperienced managers. Instead, their growing obsession with each other's weaknesses caused them to lose out on the strengths they each brought and created additional problems that only put additional strain on the relationship and made them less effective at completing the work that needed to get done. Even worse, as they blamed each other, fear and worry pervaded their relationship, and they further perpetuated a pattern of not expressing their differences.

ᕍ

As Howie had ominously predicted, when the deadline finally arrived, the technical consultants did not deliver. The launch was pushed back several weeks. It was finally set for a Wednesday, and to ensure it would happen smoothly, the consulting firm sent two consultants from their Denver office to Versity on Monday morning. At first, it looked promising that the launch would occur on the rescheduled date. However, the website ended up not being launched until Saturday morning, after a week of sleepless nights. As soon as the site was launched, everyone went home to get some rest, including the consultants, who flew back to their homes in Denver.

When Howie woke up later that Saturday afternoon, he found that the site was not working. There was a bug. And as he had feared, the consultants were gone. Worse yet, their contract had expired, and they wanted no more responsibility. All Howie could do was call his tech team together to try to fix their nonfunctioning website in a programming language they barely knew.

CHAPTER EIGHT

No One's Explaining,
No One's Asking

W HEN VERSITY was located in Michigan, people came to work when they woke up and left when they were too tired to do any more. They wore whatever they wanted and acted however they wanted. The office was a mess; boxes and cans piled up. The folks from Michigan cared little about order, cleanliness, or decor. Posting lecture notes to the website, running promotions, and acquiring new users consumed them. From their perspective, being obsessed with the work itself was at the very essence of their success; it made Versity more than just another company.

The professional managers, however, could not stand an office that lacked structure, order, and cleanliness. Dave, the new vice president of product development, told me, "If you want to be a dominant player, you have to look it. You need to blow people away and make them afraid to compete. You need to look and feel like a more successful place." Sharon, the new vice president of human resources, believed she needed to build an infrastructure where none existed. She was concerned that without human resource policies and benefits in place, Versity would not be able to attract new people. Meanwhile, Jim, the new chief financial officer, was shocked to find that college kids were running around with the corporate credit card. He could not believe that such young employees were trusted in this way. He was busy worrying about creating a credit card policy, setting up accounting procedures and payroll, and standardizing salaries and stock options.

The founders watched quietly as these policies and procedures went into effect. They said nothing. A few months earlier they had been charging thousands of dollars to their personal credit cards to cover Versity's expenses. Suddenly, the new credit card policy required them never to use the company credit card for personal items, even if they intended to reimburse the company immediately. Moreover, if they did not hand in all of their receipts within a two-week window, their cards would be revoked. Similarly, they had not taken a day off since they founded the company, often working around the clock. When Sharon announced a vacation policy that allowed them to accrue time off at ten hours per month, they could only laugh in disbelief. A constant refrain among the Michigan gang was, "You have to be kidding."

While the professional managers were working hard to create order out of chaos, they were also trying to be careful not to go too far. They told me they were holding themselves back. They realized that Versity was a start-up and required greater flexibility than the established firms for which they had previously worked. They told me, too, that they did not want to make the place "too stuffy." Rather, they wanted to keep it "relaxed," "fun," "casual." They just wanted the headquarters to be "a little less like a fraternity house, and more like an office."

But the new protocols made the founders bristle. They resented the layers of bureaucracy, making the company unnecessarily "old and stodgy." One night Daniel complained to Howie and me, "Politics are creeping in. The company is becoming more corporate. It's more political, less rugged, down to earth." Howie added, "It used to be flat around here. Now this place is becoming fluffy with hierarchy. There are managers around, people you have to prove yourself to; there are formal work hours and times you are expected to be here."

The founders became increasingly unmotivated and lacked their old passion. They no longer enjoyed being at work nor did they feel the tremendous dedication to the company they once had.

They worried whether the professional managers knew what they were doing. They voiced their concerns, but only to one another. By gossiping among themselves, they temporarily vented their frustrations. However, they didn't take responsibility to explore their differences, and as a result they missed an opportunity to enable both sides to learn about the other's issues.

The professional managers had no idea that their actions were causing so much concern. It never occurred to them to reassure the founders or explain to them why they were making all these changes. They just assumed that the changes made good sense and that the founders understood their importance.

ॐ

As the founders' concerns about the professional managers became increasingly fierce, they decided to meet just the four of them for the first time since arriving in California. The meeting took place over dinner at an upscale Italian restaurant in downtown Palo Alto. Howie began the conversation: "They [the professional managers] don't understand culture. They think that culture is paintball and barbecues. They don't understand that culture is who we are, how we do things, the speed and passion with which we work. It is our drive and motivation. They are killing the culture."

Daniel asked, "As a founders' group, are we too quiet? Should we unify more as a group?"

Clyde chimed in, "There are certain things that are not getting addressed. But we cannot tell the VCs. We cannot tell them that the management is not good enough. What should we do?"

Clyde began to assess the new managers one by one. "The fact is that Sharon cannot hire. She has not brought in a single useful tech person. Who has she helped hire? No one in COPs [campus operations], no one in business development, no one in tech, no one in product development, no one in marketing. She has not hired a single person. We need a demon for hiring, and Sharon is too slow for this job."

Daniel joked, "She organized our health plan and our vacation policy."

Howie chuckled but then turned serious. "These deficiencies are threatening the success of our company."

Clyde went on, "Look at Jim. He lacks the killer instinct. He does not even know how to get us into a bank. Christ, I have the [expletive] connections to do it. I am only twenty-two, and I can do a better job than these people. Sharon is too slow. Where is the action? I can hire better. I have already. And Jim? I can do his role, too. I've already done it."

The founders were beginning to question their managers' core competencies. Howie in particular had already fretted greatly about their lack of technical expertise. Now, however, the founders were questioning not just their technical savvy but the very competencies the managers were hired to bring to the company. The founders worried that their professional managers either didn't understand, or were not willing to attend to, what the company really needed.

The founders identified problem after problem. They kept focusing on their concerns.

"The whole company needs to be pumped up," noted Clyde.

Daniel added, "Look at the big picture—there's no fun here at all anymore. There's no family culture. The family culture is *dead*. It's like a new company around here."

Howie agreed. "People just don't care. They don't like being in the office anymore. It's not a friendly atmosphere. It's too sterile."

They reminisced about the good old days and all the water fights and games.

As the evening was winding down, Howie said, "We need to think of some positive ways to turn this around. What are they? We need to figure out some definitive steps to get there. We need change."

This led to a pivotal conversation about what the founders believed was the core problem: They had handed over control of their company expecting that professional managers would know how to run it better than they did. As it turned out, however, these managers did not know all the things that the founders had expected them to know.

This was a tremendous shift in perception. Up to this point, the founders had been convinced that their professional managers knew something the founders did not know and that therefore the founders had to defer to them. Suddenly, the founders began to think otherwise. This thought deeply troubled them, and they started to wonder why they even had had to bring in professional managers.

꒰

Although getting together to discuss these issues among themselves provided the founders a source of support and a starting point from which they could have built an effective coalition to try to change the situation, they stopped short of taking advantage of their potential power. Instead, they focused their energy on complaining about the professional managers and their situation. At one point, Howie did remark that they needed to think of "positive ways to turn this around." However, they continued to blame the professional managers, never stepping back to ask about their own role in the process or how they could communicate their concerns to the professional managers in a way that the latter might be able to hear and understand them—and potentially do something differently as a result.

※

As the founders were busy worrying about the professional managers, they never realized how much their suspicions were aggravating the managers' feelings toward them. The professional managers felt pressure to act as though they were leaders, guides—the ones with all the answers. Meanwhile, they were increasingly convinced that they had stepped into something that was in much worse shape than they had expected. However, they felt uncomfortable admitting their lack of knowledge as to how to fix all these problems. Rather, as leaders, they felt it was their responsibility to know what to do, or to at least act as if they did.

To admit what they did not know would have required the courage to break the norms governing what a leader is expected to say and do. To find the courage to do so is easier in a relationship founded on trust and respect. The professional managers, however, had built no such relationship with the founders. On the contrary, they were growing increasingly mistrustful and disrespectful of one another. This context made the professional managers all the more self-protective and therefore less comfortable admitting what they did not know.

Instead, feeling insecure about their own lack of knowledge, the professional managers blamed the founders for expecting them to know everything and ensure that everything flowed flawlessly. The professional managers concluded that the founders did not have the maturity to form reasonable expectations of them. A constant refrain among the professional managers was, "If only the founders had worked before, they would realize that everything does not always happen smoothly."

The professional managers, much like the founders, ended up blaming the other group, the founders in their case, instead of taking responsibility for their problems and trying to think proactively about how they could most effectively work together. Indeed, no discussion ever took place about what they expected from one another. There was not a single discussion among the management team about who did what. They were so focused on one crisis after the next that no one ever took the time to step back and explore their roles, responsibilities, or relationships.

꙳

After their conversation over dinner, the founders decided they had to speak up. They told Peter that the office was becoming too professional. They reminded him of the Wednesday company dinner they used to have back in Michigan that drew everyone together. In response, Peter decided to reinstate the Wednesday dinner.

Whenever the professional managers heard resistance from the founders, they tried to accommodate. When the founders later confided in Dave additional concerns about the culture, he encouraged them to again share their issues with Peter. That evening, the four founders plus Dave went over to Peter's house. Howie described their intentions: "We went over to Peter's because we wanted things to be different."

Hearing their concerns about the culture, but without pushing to understand better why they felt the way that they did or what was really bothering them, Peter decided to set up a fraternity system. Peter and Dave had both often described to me their own impressions of the old days at Versity back in Michigan as "fraternity-like." Now Peter proposed that the four founders would each have a role. Howie would be the fraternity president. Clyde would work on attracting new young people to the company, as the rush chair. Daniel would be the social chair—doing things like organizing the Wednesday dinner. Aaron would be in charge of introducing new people when they joined the company.

To the founders, this modification was seemingly quite silly. It did nothing to change the bigger problem about their culture. But they said nothing to Peter or Dave about it. To ask for further change, the founders would have had to acknowledge the inadequacy of the proposed *patch*.

By putting these roles in place, Peter had again managed to muffle the founders' discontent without addressing their real differences about the company's culture and their even deeper differences in expectations about the role of professional managers. But as we've seen over and over, *patching* does not resolve tension—it only further buries it. Howie said to me, "I know they are trying, but I just do not think they get it." Indeed, because the founders thought the managers were actually trying, their failure was all the more alarming. The founders viewed the insufficiency of the managers' solutions as confirmation of the professional managers' inability to understand the founders and the needs of their company.

The managers, however, were unaware of the founders' increasing skepticism. They convinced themselves that by adding dinners and titles they were responding to what the founders wanted. Most of all, the superficial actions kept deeper, more problematic issues—about how to run the company, what the culture should be, and what roles each of them should play—at bay. The managers' real fears concerned having to admit that they did not know all the answers, but they worked hard to keep these fears hidden. Still unknowingly, by making only small superficial changes, the managers fueled the founders' skepticism about the managers' competence—the very thing the managers were most worried about revealing.

The larger, unnamed problems lurking beneath the surface were not being addressed. To speak out at this point felt threatening, given the norms of silence compounded by the growing discontent and disrespect. However, what those involved did not realize was that to continue to cover over these deep and growing issues, while seemingly safer at the moment, provided only temporary relief. The bigger issue was the future, because all these acts of cover-up were continuing to build on themselves, and fear and distrust in the relationship between the founders and their managers were continuing to grow at an alarming rate.

⌇

The professional managers had a good sense of what they thought Versity's direction should be. They worried, though, that the founders did not agree. Dave broached the topic at a weekly management meeting. "There is a problem that we need to address," he said. "We need to talk about the purpose of the company. We all need to be on the same page."

The discussion that followed quickly became chaotic. Everyone had an opinion on the matter. When Peter finally managed to get everyone's attention, he suggested that they devote a day solely to the topic. Jill, who had been a consultant before joining Versity as head of public relations, interjected that she had run this type of "vision meeting" many times before. She laid out a plan for how the day could go and volunteered to organize it.

⌇

Several weeks later the vision meeting was held offsite in a non-descript hotel conference room. The day started promptly at

8:00 A.M. Peter opened the meeting by saying, "Our goal is to end up on the same page. We are currently moving in an unclear direction, and we need to be more clear." They talked first about their personal values. Jill went around the room, asking each participant to list a value; then others were asked to come up with a definition. Howie offered "reliability." Individuals described it as "Say you will do it, and do it"; "Meets deadlines"; "You can count on them"; and "There when you need them." After defining a whole list of personal values, they moved on to discuss company values. Again they went around the room. This time they each shared three words to describe what they thought their company's values should be. When they finished, they had eighteen different values on the list. They spent the next hour talking about these eighteen values and trying to narrow them down to a more manageable number. They came to agree on a list of eight: "results-driven; passion about what we do; integrity; respect; team/people/community; fast; fun; focused." They left it at that.

The discussions were meant as a vehicle to share personal perspectives and to try to get different opinions heard. However, that was not always what happened. At one point, Peter was talking about the valuation drivers and the key focus of the organization. Clyde brought up the importance of registered users. Peter snapped, "Clyde, you are talking about strategy, and we need to stay on topic." To Clyde it was not at all clear what was meant by "strategy" versus "vision," but he instantly became silent.

At another point, after creating a long list of stakeholders, they quickly realized that they could not meet so many different demands. Dave stated, "We have to favor some over others. We have to maintain a balance as a management team." They started talking about the need to prioritize stakeholders and how to do that. They started to disagree. Jill intervened: "The point is not to come to closure. It is just to help us raise awareness of our different constituents. Lots of work comes out of a meeting like this. We will need to sort through all of this. Our first step is just to get it all out." She effectively tabled the topic for the day.

The final exercise began at 3:30 P.M. Jill set the scene: "It is 2001. Two years from now. Versity has just been selected for the Twenty-first Century Award. You are about to be on a nationally televised award show, and you will go on in a few minutes to accept the award. It will air in Europe, a market in which you are not yet operating. You are about to go on and describe what Versity is and what the company does. Write down your thoughts. Remember, it's two years from now." For the next ten minutes everyone scribbled notes on a piece of paper.

Once they were finished, each read their description. Having heard from everyone, Rob—who had come from Michigan with the original team—said, "I like Clyde's." After some brief discussion, Jill asked Clyde to read his again. He read, "Versity.com is the premier academic resource on the Internet. Anytime someone wants to get information to help them write papers, do research, look up famous professors, get class notes, or study, they come to us. It is the most heavily trafficked site for college students and for professors. It has partnerships with all the major information providers, and it has the largest database of information available anywhere. On the Internet, Versity also has tools and products that professors at universities everywhere embrace and that improve the value of education for all."

A discussion followed about how much they needed to target professors specifically, offering products to them. Peter was adamant: "We need to develop relations with professors." He told them about an online education company, IZIO, that he had learned about the previous day. Peter described how IZIO had developed a new way to enable professors to more effectively use technology to manage their courses. He told them how IZIO enables professors to do things like facilitate online discussions among students and post anything from syllabi to assignments to announcements on a website available only to the professor's own students. He explained how IZIO targets professors but in the process attracts all of the professor's students to the website. When professors use the product, it becomes a requirement of the course for all of their students. Peter confessed to the group, "Seeing IZIO has scared me."

More than being just an effective way to indirectly attract students, Peter feared that professors had real power to put them out of business. He felt strongly that professors had to become their core audience. He cautioned the group that faculty had real power, and that they had to find a way to appeal to them.

The founders, however, were much less inclined to make faculty their primary customer. As Daniel put it, "We went after the masses. We should continue to focus on students. We know and have established that we still must minimally appease the faculty."

At this point Dave piped up: "Vision does not require us to make this choice. We want to be the premier academic website, and that is our vision. If that means that faculty are part of it, then that will be the case. We need to keep our eye on it and do it if necessary. If it takes working with faculty to be the premier academic website, then that is what we will do."

Dave's comment raised a further discussion of whether being the premier academic website was indeed their vision. Some agreed. Others, however, felt it was about profit, number of visitors to their website, or education. Peter intervened: "This is not about our vision. It will open up a whole other discussion for another day." Indeed, whenever there was indication of disagreement, someone quickly *glossed over* that difference by labeling the issue "strategy" or something else that was not to be addressed at a "vision meeting."

The definition of vision had very little consistency. Anything on which they disagreed became, by definition, *not* vision, and therefore something to be discussed on another day. Despite the constant shifts in what the concept of vision meant, no one said a word. Anytime someone tried to silence a conversation, they succeeded. The group simply acquiesced and moved on.

At the end of the discussion, Jill handed each person a hotdog-shaped balloon, the type that clowns give out at the circus. She asked everyone to express their observations about the day, saying whether their expectations had been met and how they felt at the moment. Hal, the acting head of marketing, went first. "My expectations were met," he said. "Jill, you did a great job. We made some great progress today. It feels great. I am excited . . . passionate . . . committed to the future." Dave, head of product development, continued: "The consistency of vision and purpose is good to hear. We are pretty similar in what we are thinking. We are not automatons, but consistency is good." Jim, the CFO, boasted: "I am happy. I thought today was going to be a lot uglier. I expected battles. Yet things were remarkably consistent." Peter added: "It was a good starting point. Jill did a good job keeping us moving. I enjoyed today." Similarly, the company's founders expressed relief at the consistency they had heard. Clyde sounded pleased: "After today I am more comfortable that we are all on the same page." And Howie shared: "It was neat to have everyone in the same room together. I was quiet because I wanted to hear what others had to say. I wanted to hear from the new people, with new ideas and new perspectives. It seems we all pretty much agree on what is going on. Thank you."

⌁

On some level, the professional managers and the founders were well aware of their differences. But they had so successfully silenced themselves and one another at the vision meeting that they managed to convey that there was consensus when there was not. Both the founders and professional managers had played a part in this construction. And each person's final reflection on the meeting only further reinforced the false sense of consensus.

Perhaps most revealing, after each person had read their personal version of the vision statement, the group had never examined the differences in perspectives revealed by their various statements. Rather they focused on one, Clyde's, and even whittled it down to avoid controversy. In the end, they managed to conclude the day on a note of euphoria, having temporarily suspended their awareness of the pretend nature of all of this seeming consensus.

The list of what did not get discussed at the vision meeting was far more impressive than what did. The founders never aired their concerns about their managers as leaders. The managers never voiced their concerns about being expected to know all the answers. Nothing was decided about how to prioritize faculty versus students as the customer. No one acknowledged that these differences could have real significance to their working relationship.

The managers and the founders willingly engaged in the effort to avoid conflict, perpetuating a norm of silence that had been set in motion in Peter's first days in the company and continued to gain support. Under the aegis of "getting it all out," they managed to so fill the day as to prevent all but the most superficial discussion of problematic issues. Indeed, nothing had been done to designate that this meeting was somehow different from a normal management meeting. However, in a group in which the norm was not to express differences, if people suddenly wanted to have an open discussion of their differences, someone would have had to take responsibility, go first, and express their genuine thoughts and feelings. As soon as people tried to act in the desired way—expressing their differences— they would have further needed to feel that there was a shared desire to hear and explore these different perspectives.

꒳

After the vision meeting, the founders and the professional managers continued to work together, but with very different perspectives about the company and its focus. The founders' primary concern was increasing the number of people who used their website. They worried greatly that they did not have the user acquisition numbers needed to succeed in the dot-com economy. The founders focused on doing whatever they could to increase these numbers.

Peter, in the meantime, started looking further into IZIO, trying to find out how serious a threat it posed, whether Versity could acquire IZIO, and whether such a purchase might help appease disgruntled faculty. Peter quickly recognized that IZIO was providing faculty a set of Web tools that the faculty actually wanted; and any faculty who used this product automatically brought every student in their class to the site, because it became part of taking the class. Peter saw huge potential in IZIO's business model.

While the founders focused on user numbers and Peter focused on learning more about IZIO, they all persisted in their silence, acting as if they agreed—despite pursuing different paths. No one revisited their points of disagreement or proposed gathering again to tackle the tough questions that had been tabled. Under the guise of consensus, it was all the more difficult to have such a conversation.

꒳

Although Versity struggled, it did manage to hit 100,000 users. Howie and Aaron went out to buy champagne to celebrate. Peter instructed them to buy expensive champagne, emphasizing, "This is a big occasion." In Howie's mind, this was not such a good day. It was not that it was a bad day. Although he was delighted that Versity had finally hit 100,000 users, he felt it would have been much better if they had hit that number two months earlier, as they had originally forecasted.

Initially, the goal for the semester had been 275,000 to 500,000 users. Now, with the end of the semester fast approaching, they had only a month to more than double their achievement if they were going to attain that goal. The founders felt immense pressure to improve their numbers. They believed that all the disruptions—moving to California, upgrading the site, hiring professional managers, and shifting roles—had taken a toll. The founders feared the consequences, knowing that this was a critical semester and that they had not achieved their potential. They were well aware of the importance of timing, in terms of aggregating enough users to raise money at a reasonable valuation. They wondered why the professional managers didn't understand how vital it was to aggregate users as quickly as possible. But, perceiving that it was best to say nothing and just keep moving forward, the founders went along with Peter's plan and celebrated their progress to date.

Although Peter never told the founders, the only reason he saw for celebrating 100,000 users was that he knew user numbers mattered to them. He knew it was an important metric in their minds. However, secretly, he had a very different set of concerns. He worried greatly about the image of the company and the reactions of the professors, noting, "I still like the original idea, but with the campus issues, we have no choice but to find a way to refocus to be more professor friendly." He believed that the campus problems were fundamental and that if they could not find a way to redirect the company to address these problems, they were in serious trouble, far beyond user numbers. He added, out of earshot of the rest of the company, "In the end, whether we have 100,000 or 200,000 users is not going to affect our valuation. That is not the issue. The issue is these university problems. It's like a house on stilts in quicksand. That is the problem. Not the number of users. We have grown too quickly. We have expanded to schools when we knew we were just picking a fight, and yet we still went. It is those issues we need to address."

Peter believed that they could try to knock off the campus problems one by one. Indeed, they were having much success each time they went to a campus and spent the necessary time to explain their intentions to the faculty and administration. However, he was also convinced that the process was taking way too long; it was simply not feasible with the speed required to raise money. Peter instead was looking for new alternatives to evolve the company into new markets so that campus problems would not seem so large.

Still, acting as if achieving 100,000 users were indeed an important milestone on a critical path, the founders and Peter joined together to celebrate their progress to date—progress that to the founders was totally insufficient and that to Peter was totally irrelevant. However, by all taking part in the celebration, they each avoided having to confront the deeper issue of why none of them actually thought this event worthy of a celebration.

༄

When Peter approached the IZIO founders, he learned they were struggling financially. IZIO had been created the previous year by three Stanford graduate students. They had signed up forty faculty members at Stanford to buy IZIO's product, but they needed more money to help them further expand their company.

Peter was ecstatic. He knew instantaneously that this was a huge opportunity. IZIO was desperate for money. He was desperate for a path to move away from notes. He had been looking for a way to work with professors rather than just sneaking into their classes. Suddenly, IZIO could provide Versity something that directly helped the faculty. Peter believed he had found a way out of Versity's most vexing problem. IZIO provided a new direction, a way to be faculty-friendly while still aggregating students.

A special board meeting was called to discuss the potential acquisition of IZIO. The board members—with the exception of Howie—readily agreed with Peter that IZIO was a worthwhile investment. They agreed to offer IZIO $750,000 dollars and 15 percent of the combined company in stock.

Not surprisingly, the Versity founders were not happy about this deal. It had nothing to do with the direction in which they were trying to move their company. Moreover, from their perspective, it seemed that they were substantially overpaying for IZIO. Howie explained to me, "What we are getting for 15 percent of the company is three employees, a new technology, and a relationship with a prestigious university [Stanford]." As for the relationship with Stanford, "The deal is not even done yet. And even if it does go through, IZIO is expecting to service sixty professors next semester. It is definitely not as if they have the whole campus wrapped up." Then there were the problems with IZIO's technology. Howie was convinced that the IZIO code would have to be rewritten. It too was in Cold Fusion. Howie said, "They face the same types of scalability issues that we did. There goes at least another $250,000 to have the code rewritten." He summed up his point about their technology: "Basically we are getting no technology, because it has to be redone." Howie did think IZIO's technology was interesting, but the fact that it had to be redone convinced him that Versity's tech team could build it just as easily themselves. There was also a further issue as to how they would find the resources to staff both companies. They couldn't even find enough good people to staff Versity.

Neither Howie nor Clyde appreciated the upside of the deal. They did not see why Peter believed that IZIO offered them so much value. Not comprehending the severity of their situation—at least as Peter saw it—they had no reason to appreciate the genius of Peter's escape route from Versity's campus problems: winning over professors by providing services useful to them. And Peter never tried to explain why he believed the resistance at the universities could prove fatal for Versity's business model and why this deal had the potential to save them. Since his earliest panic about the business model when Princeton University had changed its honor code to forbid students using online lecture notes, Peter had masterfully concealed his concerns from the founders.

Lacking this fundamental understanding of Peter's perspective, Howie and Clyde were genuinely confused and distressed. From their perspective, Versity had failed miserably to hit its user goals. And nothing had been done to ensure that it would not happen again. They thought Versity should be reacting and changing to address the situation with user numbers. They did not understand how Peter's desire to acquire IZIO helped to address what they saw as their fundamental weakness.

Despite pressure from the venture capitalists to keep the founders happy and aware of the founders' resistance to the IZIO deal, Peter was still convinced that acquiring IZIO was necessary. As he explained to me, IZIO provided the critical new direction Versity so desperately needed. He considered making IZIO *the* central aspect of the business, shifting the whole company's focus to faculty and dropping lecture notes completely. He reasoned, however, that he should at least give notes a try.

Peter still believed notes could provide an additional source of revenue. IZIO made money by selling products to professors. In the process, however, all of the professors' students were attracted to the website. Yet, it was not appropriate to sell products to the students on the IZIO site. To do so would entail mixing education and consumerism. Just as one never sees advertisements in a college textbook, professors did not want any advertising on a website that they required their students to visit. However, what online lecture notes provided was an opportunity to transfer students to a different site. Students could have the option to click on a button on the IZIO site if they wanted online lecture notes. In doing so, they would be transferred to the Versity site. Once on the Versity site, it would be more appropriate to sell products to the students. Peter therefore reasoned that it would be worth trying to pursue both IZIO and Versity. However, he further assured himself that if the campus problems persisted, they could always do away with notes and pursue just IZIO.

つ

Soon after Christmas, the IZIO founders moved into the Versity office.

Peter was a cheerleader for IZIO, showing great enthusiasm and support for all of its accomplishments. He directed Versity's professional managers to focus most of their attention on IZIO and its expansion. Moreover, he allocated whatever resources he could to enable the IZIO team to fly around the country and give demonstrations of their products to professors.

People involved with IZIO were working hard to find professors interested in their faculty website. People involved in Versity were focused on achieving the maximum campus presence, acquiring as many users as possible, and exploring the potential opportunity of charging for notes. They all were working extremely hard. They were not, however, working together or attempting to create any synergies. People worked either for Versity or IZIO; no one worked for both.

Indeed, several times one of the IZIO founders, Ned, approached Mark, the head of campus operations for Versity, with the intent of asking some of Versity's campus managers to also act as sales representatives for IZIO on their respective campuses. Each time Ned approached Mark, however, he got the same response: "Not now." Ned recounted with great frustration, "Mark always says it's not a good time. They just do not want us to use their COMs [campus operations managers]."

Instead of energy being pooled to best address the interests of the overarching company, energy was divided into separate spheres—Versity and IZIO.

CHAPTER NINE

Bad Endings

COLLEGECLUB, an online company focused on creating communities of college students, expressed interest in acquiring Versity. CollegeClub's management wanted to do so quickly, before CollegeClub filed to go public early in the new year. Peter was intrigued, and the possibility of doing a deal with CollegeClub spurred him to call up a range of other big, related sites and explore their interest in doing a deal as well.

꒰ꔛ꒱

Late one night in a conference room at the Versity office, the four founders gathered to discuss the potential sale of their company. Clyde opened the conversation: "I believe it is in our best interest to sell. I know that is truly pathetic to say, but that is what I think." Howie commented, "It certainly is a lot earlier than I would have expected."

Clyde added, "We do not have what it takes. Our burn rate is too high. We don't have the traffic or the momentum or the management to expand as aggressively as we would have to if we are to succeed. We should sell and take the risk out of it. We no longer control our destiny. We have lost control. Since we do not know what will happen, the best we can do is try to ensure against failure. Joining with a company that is about to have an IPO [initial public offering] will minimize our risk."

Howie, with shock and despair, gasped, "It also makes us the *acquired!*" At that, they all paused.

Clyde eventually continued, "Too much is not going well. IZIO is not being effectively staffed. People are not good enough in this company. They are not motivated enough. We have no choice but to sell."

Howie took a deep breath. "We too [messed] up, as board members and founders. We didn't say, 'Listen, this needs to be fixed, you need to focus on this.' We assumed Peter knew what he was doing. We thought the problems were obvious and would be addressed. Everyone told us we had to bring in senior people and trust them. To an extent I believe it is true, but maybe we didn't have to buy into it as much. We should have had more hesitation when things were not going well."

There was a sense among the founders that the most important thing, running the company—its culture, internal organization, and people management—had somehow fallen through the cracks.

Daniel noted, "Peter is good at schmoozing and addressing external matters. He does not manage the internals of the company, though. He leaves that to Dave. But Dave is not aggressive enough."

Howie added, "The problem is that neither Dave nor Peter is in charge of running the show. It is like a ship without anyone at the helm."

Despite agreement about the problems, Howie and Clyde could not agree as to whether they should sell the company. Whereas Clyde thought they had no choice but to sell, Howie worried that they were giving up too easily and that selling Versity was premature. No resolution satisfied them both.

Finally, Clyde suggested that they call Kevin O'Connor, the CEO of DoubleClick, who had remained a key advisor. He was someone they both continued to trust and respect.

༄

After detailing the situation to Kevin, Clyde asked, "What do you think we should do?" Kevin was surprised to hear that they were having problems with Peter. After a long silence, he responded, "You should probably sell." It was as if the judge had just issued the final death sentence, leaving nothing more to be said.

After they hung up, no one was quite sure what to say. Trying to reassure themselves that selling was their only option, Daniel noted, "If it really was only one thing, we would sit down with Peter and tell him. We would tell him that he should do the external stuff and the founders would do all the internal stuff." Clyde, unable to restrain himself, joked, "Yeah, right, he just made you social chair."

༄

The more the professional managers thought about selling the company, the more positively they favored it. For them, and Peter in particular, selling was a way to escape campus resistance, to grow bigger in a consolidating market, and to access much-needed financial resources.

To Peter, selling showed his good sense to get out before Versity got destroyed. Peter believed that if the company could effectively integrate IZIO, it would stand a chance. But as Peter reflected on the impasse he had reached with the founders, he reasoned that they had no choice but to sell the company.

༄

Because they had never resolved or even clarified their differences, the founders still did not understand Peter's view that the campus resistance posed a severe problem. Peter, in the meantime, could not comprehend how the founders could remain so naive about these problems. In this vacuum, both sides continued to make increasingly more hostile accusations about the other. The founders started to suspect that Peter had an ulterior motive, that he had always intended to sell the company. Peter interpreted the founders' continued resistance as confirming evidence of their incredible stubbornness and their unwillingness to give up control.

Originally, the founders and their new professional managers had silenced themselves in hopes of preserving their relationships above all else. Now both sides silenced themselves because they had lost so much respect for one another that it was not worth the effort to try to make things work between them. They had reached the breaking point, continuing to work together only in a state of *withdrawal*. It was all they could do to go on working side by side, each on different projects, in pursuit of different goals.

Still, no one said a word about these issues to one another. They all tried to maintain a front of friendly relations. They continued to joke around and engage in social chitchat. It was only behind closed doors that the bitterness reached new heights.

⤳

Soon after CollegeClub made its initial offer to acquire Versity, a second company, Snowball, also began to show interest. As soon as Snowball expressed interest, the members of the Versity management team all agreed that they would much prefer to sell to Snowball. They believed Snowball had more potential as a business, and they felt more comfortable with its culture. Peter described the people at CollegeClub as "ex-surfers from San Diego," whereas Snowball was more "the MBA type." Snowball was filled with Harvard and Stanford MBAs, making Peter feel more at home. The founders also preferred to sell to Snowball, not so much because of what they knew about Snowball as because of their dislike for CollegeClub. Back in Michigan they used to have a sign posted in the office that read, "CollegeClub is irrelevant, Collegestudent is so irrelevant." Making College-Club all the less appealing, it had recently completed an acquisition of Collegestudent. Howie expressed his feelings toward CollegeClub when he told me, "I just don't respect the site. It's a [expletive] company. It's a big mess, all based on chat. It's trivial." He further noted, "I just don't feel like they have a long-run vision; they are not the ones who will be changing the world."

Despite everyone's preference to sell to Snowball, Peter established a bidding war to maximize their valuation. Over the four weeks of negotiating that followed, everyone's clear desire remained to sell to Snowball. Then, on February 1—one day before the date on which Peter had promised to reveal Versity's final decision—Peter, along with several other members of the management team, visited both companies one last time and on this final trip discovered new information. The next morning, Peter reported in a management meeting that Snowball planned to allocate money based on how many users Versity acquired. This meant that Versity would be expected to create something with nothing and even worse, with someone always looking over their shoulders. In contrast, at CollegeClub, he reported, "They really seem committed to the academic space. They are impressive in their commitment to what they are trying to do. By no means are they out of the woods with the volume of work that needs to get done—but they have commitment."

Expecting everyone to trust his judgment, he asked his management team rhetorically, "Anyone against selling to College-Club?" Howie, having not been part of the prior day's visits, but having visited CollegeClub himself only a few days earlier, was shocked by the sudden turn of events. After a long silence, Howie spoke up, questioning what had changed Peter's mind. Rather than answer his question, Peter *suppressed* Howie one final time, telling him, "The board told us to use our gut, and our gut has come out telling us CollegeClub. The fact that Snowball wants us to do it their way makes us realize that we will have more influence at CollegeClub."

Nothing more was said on the topic.

Although it may appear that the managers explored two options, dragging out the decision for several months, in reality they never seriously explored the possibility of selling to CollegeClub. Initially, they explored the question of whether to sell, and from the moment that Snowball made its initial offer, they were in unanimous agreement on their preference to sell to Snowball. When selling to Snowball suddenly became undesirable, there was no backup plan; no other options had ever been seriously considered. Yet, given the incredible pressure to go fast and make a decision, at this point one of the most important decisions in the company's history was made after gathering hardly any additional information, without considering each person's perspective, and without consulting any outside advisors. The company had fallen into a self-made speed trap.

༒

That afternoon, Versity signed a letter of intent to sell to CollegeClub for CollegeClub stock estimated to be worth $125 million.

The founders were devastated. They saw it as "an order-of-magnitude problem." They thought they should be worth an order of magnitude more than the $10 million the stock they would now each own was estimated to be worth, and for that they blamed Peter and the managers he had hired. From the founders' perspective, it was the new managers who had caused them to have to sell the company long before they should have sold.

At the same time, the professional managers, and Peter in particular, attributed the sale to the founders' unwillingness to accept the problems the company faced and their inability to be flexible and adaptable in ways that would enable them to address these problems. Each blamed the other. No one recognized the role he personally had played in creating an outcome with which none of them was satisfied.

ॐ

Six weeks passed. During this time, CollegeClub managers made many trips back and forth between San Diego and Palo Alto, exploring the internal workings of Versity. In the process, they discovered that the founders and the professional managers had little respect for one another and didn't collaborate. Increasingly concerned about the potential explosion of this situation, the CollegeClub managers decided they had to get rid of Peter and the managers he had hired.

Since Peter's employment contract stated that Versity had to be located within fifteen miles of Palo Alto, CollegeClub decided to require—for the deal to close—that the company relocate to San Diego. This way, CollegeClub's senior managers reasoned, the desired effect would be achieved: Peter would not move, and they would be able to oversee Versity's daily operations themselves.

No one at Versity had an inkling this was coming.

Suddenly faced with the news of the required move, late on Friday afternoon, March 16, 2000, the Versity management team gathered to discuss the situation. They decided to hold an emergency meeting the following morning with the whole company.

Seeming quite anxious, Peter reported in the meeting the

next morning: "We were informed yesterday that CollegeClub is uncomfortable with the Versity team working well up here [in Palo Alto]. To get the confidence they need, the only way is for the group to move to San Diego." Peter struggled with how to phrase things and paused to think at different points. His hesitation conveyed his lack of clarity about what was happening. He continued, "I cannot tell you if we say 'forget it' that they won't do the deal, but I believe there is a 90-plus probability that they won't." He shrugged his shoulders and continued to tremble. "I cannot tell you whether, if we don't do the deal, the VCs will continue to fund in the capacity they are doing now." He further speculated, "Even if they do fund us, I don't know what it will cost in terms of the equity we would have to give up." He did make it clear about himself: "I am not moving." Expressing his own surprise, he told them, "I have already conveyed that to CollegeClub, but apparently that is not a deal stopper." He also explained he had to "deliver a paper this afternoon that lists the names of those who will move and those who will not." He admitted, "I am terribly upset, but it is what it is, and we will all try to deal with it as best we can."

⌇

Peter never realized what had precipitated the sudden demand that Versity relocate to San Diego. He believed that the College-Club managers had become concerned that he would start up the academic unit and then leave them without a manager to run the place. It never occurred to him that the managers at College-Club were forcing this move to oust him.

It did, however, occur to Peter that maybe he should stop the deal. He again wondered about the possibility of just pursuing IZIO. Indeed, he went so far as to write a business plan and talk to Versity's venture capitalists about it. However, when Peter presented the idea to the founders, given the option of pursuing only IZIO or selling to CollegeClub, the founders still did not understand Peter's rationale for focusing only on IZIO, and so they decided that between what they saw as two bad options, selling was the better one. Peter therefore told his management team that although the possibility of getting more funding and pursuing only IZIO existed, it was to be their backup plan, to be followed only if the deal with CollegeClub fell through. "The founders want to sell, and the VCs will support what the founders want. We should do what we can within reason to make it happen."

᠅

The negotiation dragged on for weeks. On April 19, 2000, ten weeks after the signing of the letter of intent and sixteen weeks after CollegeClub had made its initial offer, the deal went through. Versity was sold to CollegeClub. That afternoon, CollegeClub filed to go public.

᠅

Six weeks later, the founders and most of their employees moved to San Diego. Neither Peter nor any of the other professional managers went with them. Immediately upon Versity's arrival in San Diego, it became apparent that CollegeClub was struggling. The recent events in the market had made it almost impossible for companies to go public unless they showed a profit.[1] CollegeClub was not profitable. The company needed to find ways quickly to generate revenue and cut costs. They started laying off both Versity and CollegeClub employees. Within their first week in San Diego, eleven of Versity's twenty-eight employees who had made the move were let go.

At first it seemed like CollegeClub would have only one major layoff. But a few weeks later, more people were let go.

Then the layoffs just kept on happening. More and more people were being laid off or just quitting. In July, Clyde, Daniel, and Aaron were laid off. Howie was the only one retained, because CollegeClub desperately needed his technical abilities. Once the others were let go, however, Howie could not stand being there alone, and so he quit. Within a month, CollegeClub failed to make payroll and filed for bankruptcy. On August 22, 2000, less than three months after Versity had moved to San Diego, the combined company was bankrupt. The founders were left with nothing but the experiences they had shared.

AFTERWORD

In early September, two months after leaving CollegeClub, Howie planned a trip to New York City. He called Kevin O'Connor and asked if they could meet.

A week later they met for lunch. Kevin told Howie that since Howie had called, he'd been tossing around an idea: How about the Versity founders move to New York and start another company? Kevin would put up the money. He even volunteered his summer home in the Hamptons as a place where the founders could live.

When Kevin asked Howie whom he would want to work with from Versity, Howie immediately responded, "Clyde." Kevin wanted to know about Daniel and Aaron, but Howie told him that he and Clyde worked best together.

Kevin and Howie bantered about what type of company they would start. Another Internet company? A software company? They left it that Howie would talk to Clyde and get back to Kevin.

When Howie later called Clyde and told him about Kevin's idea, they shared great excitement at the thought that Kevin came up with this idea himself. Kevin's offer indicated to them that Kevin thought that what happened at Versity was not their fault. Howie proudly reported, "KO said we are true entrepreneurs, and he wants to give us another chance."

Howie and Clyde briefly discussed what to do about Daniel and Aaron. They did not want them involved. They did not feel that they had been equal partners in Versity. Indeed, they were quite critical of Daniel and Aaron—both of their work ethic and of their contributions to Versity. Still, they wondered how to handle the situation. After all, Daniel and Aaron were still their best friends. They decided to say nothing to them, at least for the time being.

During this conversation, Clyde briefly reflected to himself on the difficulties that he and Howie had had communicating with each other. Although he did not say so to Howie, Clyde was worried about Howie's issues with control.

Working again with Clyde also gave Howie reason to pause. His main concern was with how Clyde treated employees. Howie worried that Clyde expected too much out of people. But Howie, too, said nothing to Clyde.

The following week, Howie and Clyde had a conference call with Kevin. Just hearing Kevin's enthusiasm was exhilarating. Part of what Kevin told them was that he had a process, a structured process that he used to come up with the idea for his own company, DoubleClick. That there was a structured process that had led to DoubleClick made it all the more exciting.

After the call, Howie and Clyde agreed that this was an incredible opportunity. They found the idea of having Kevin on their team particularly appealing. Privately, they each worried about working with the other again. However, they each further reasoned that Kevin's involvement would make things better.

What started as a mix of excitement and concern soon evolved into overwhelming enthusiasm about the great opportunity that lay ahead. Many conversations between Howie and

Clyde transpired, but not a single one openly addressed their differences. Instead, they focused on moving forward, not looking back. And as they did, their excitement grew.

Three months after Kevin first mentioned the idea, Howie and Clyde moved into his house in the Hamptons. On Kevin's first visit, he taught them his process of brainstorming: First you come up with a list of the business problems people are facing. Next, you come up with a list of the technologies that are available. Then you try to use old technologies to solve new problems. So the process involved listing all the problems, all the technologies, and then for each problem and each technology thinking about how that technology could solve that problem. The three of them applied the process and together listed over a hundred potential ideas. They further narrowed down the ideas to eight that seemed most interesting. The next goal was to figure out whatever they could about these eight ideas. Kevin left them on their own to explore these ideas.

They read everything they could, surfed the Web, and made telephone calls. When they bounced ideas off each other, however, it always seemed to result in an argument. Instead of working off each other's energy, building on suggestions, and shaping one idea into another, they kept shooting each other down, inhibiting the creative process. Again and again they tried to engage each other in conversation, but they kept winding up at odds with each other, and frustrated.

Socially, they still spent time together. They would play pranks on each other and create fun surrounding non-work-related matters. They'd go to the beach, the movies, and the bars. But when it came to work, they stayed apart. Except when Kevin came to visit. Then the dynamic totally changed, and they became congenial, even cooperative. They shared with him all that they had learned. With Kevin around, they brainstormed together and built off each other's ideas. The ideas they reported, however, never excited Kevin. He would listen intently to what they had learned, but then always ask starkly, "What else?"

Both Howie and Clyde genuinely wanted to find something that interested Kevin, so they kept trying. They felt tremendous pressure. The clock was ticking. They had allotted three months to find an idea, and they devoted all of their waking hours to searching for it.

Once in a while Howie and Clyde would brainstorm together, but mostly they worked alone. They knew their time would be better spent if they could work together, improving and enriching each other's ideas. Neither, however, wanted to waste time fighting, and as a result they spoke less and less to each other. They found it easier to keep to themselves. The house echoed with the sounds of clicking keyboards and the occasional phone call.

Howie and Clyde kept working independently as their resentment grew increasingly intense beneath the surface. Kevin continued to visit every two or three weeks. Howie and Clyde looked forward to these meetings for an opportunity to share with him the results of their work and to brainstorm more ideas together. As time passed, however, these meetings provoked anxiety as Howie and Clyde still had produced nothing that Kevin liked. And with the increasing pressure to come up with an idea, they silenced all the more, keeping to themselves and hoping one of them would come up with something soon.

One day Howie happened to pick up a copy of *Built to Last*, which is all about the importance of having a core purpose for your company.[2] He became convinced that the fundamental problem was that he and Clyde did not agree on the purpose of their company. He worried that to Clyde the purpose was only to make money for the investors.

In the meantime, Clyde discovered a journal article that described the "proprietor" as "a person who has grown so attached to the information technology system that he feels like he personally owns it and will do anything to defend his control over it."[3] Clyde convinced himself that Howie was a "proprietor," and he feared what Howie would do to maintain control over the technology—even at the expense of the company.

The more each read about what they had come to believe was the other's "problem," the more they blamed the other, hiding from the deeper reality of what had gone wrong in their relationship, what role they had each played in the process, and how to improve their dynamic.

Just as the professional managers and the founders became incapable of seeing past their differences, Howie and Clyde now formulated their differences into barriers that could not be ignored. Their behavior, their thinking, their separation indicated that they had reached the final stage of silence—*withdrawal*—in which they no longer cared about preserving the relationship above all else.

They felt that they could not go on like this—working separately, accepting that they were at an impasse. Howie suggested that maybe bringing in a third person would help to diffuse their tension. He suggested that Mark—the former head of campus operations at Versity—would be a good third person. They both liked Mark and respected what he had accomplished at Versity. They flew him in to visit for several days. Mark met Kevin, and the four of them repeated the master brainstorming process and came up with some new ideas to investigate.

After Mark left, Clyde declared that the three of them working together again would be too similar to what they had done at Versity, and so he didn't want to hire Mark. Howie and Clyde could not agree on what to do. Howie still thought Mark would make a good hire, and Clyde presented no alternatives. Clyde decided that instead they should just call it quits. Howie, however, managed to convince Clyde that instead of calling it quits and thus having to repay Kevin the $20,000 they had already spent, Clyde should leave and let Mark take over for him. After much agonizing and bickering, Clyde decided he would rather let Mark take his place and not owe the money. So they scheduled a lunch with Kevin to share the idea.

Howie and Clyde had frequently gone into New York City to meet with Kevin, so this lunch was nothing out of the ordinary. They began as they had in the past few months, with an update on their progress and some discussion about ideas for the company. Soon, however, they broke the news. Clyde confessed to Kevin that he and Howie did not work that well together at Versity and that although they had thought they could overcome their differences, they were not succeeding. Howie then suggested that they bring in Mark to replace Clyde. All this news caught Kevin by surprise. He had had no inkling that they were struggling. Howie and Clyde had done such a good job covering over their troubles that Kevin had not realized there was a problem. Kevin asked if there was anything that could be done to fix the situation. They told him no. After letting the news sink in, Kevin said, "If that is what you want to do, I understand."

After lunch, the three of them walked through Central Park. It had become their custom to puff on cigars as they strolled along, chatting. Their conversation, as always, centered on the company and what it would become. They brainstormed and joked, considered and cajoled. A passerby would have seen three companions, intensely engaged in outwitting and impressing one another. It was only after they left Kevin that the laughter died away and the conversation stilled once again.

ༀ

Howie and Clyde parted ways. Howie continues to work with Mark and Kevin. They decided to start a chain of extreme sporting goods stores and are currently seeking funding.

Clyde spent some time in venture capital and now is back in

business school. Peter has started a new company, again focused on real estate development.

While Versity and IZIO both went bankrupt as part of CollegeClub, CollegeClub was sold out of bankruptcy to Student Advantage in the fall of 2000. At the time, IZIO was sold separately to Convene, and in the fall of 2002 Convene was further sold to Learning Technology Partners. IZIO now provides one of Learning Technology Partners' core products.[4]

༄

The question that remains is how the story of Versity might have been affected had the members found a way to effectively express their differences.

PART THREE

Escaping the Silent Spiral

CHAPTER TEN

Effectively Expressing Difference

People often fear breaking norms of silence and thus keep quiet about their differences. And in the twenty-first century, when pressure to go fast is so pervasive, the tendency to silence is all the more prevalent. However, silencing difference is extremely destructive for relationships and for work.

The goal in effectively expressing difference is to replace vicious silent spirals with virtuous spirals of speaking up. Such positive spirals perpetuate more open, honest expression of difference. The benefits of such effective expression of difference are enhanced creativity, increased learning, and healthier, more fulfilling relationships.[1]

To create virtuous rather than vicious spirals requires seeking mutual understanding. Ultimately, this quest is a shared responsibility of the people involved. Everyone needs to take responsibility for speaking and listening in a way that not only ensures clear communication but also makes it easier for others to speak up. However, if even just one person starts speaking up and listening effectively, that person will most likely be able to draw out the perspectives of the other people involved.

Instead of focusing on whose fault it is or whether it is our job or our responsibility to address the issue,[2] we need to focus instead on what can be done to move the conversation forward. We need to stop waiting to engage in the process jointly or waiting for the other person to go first. If differences are not being shared effectively, we can play a role in changing that. And the more effective we are, the more we will enable others to express themselves, and the more likely we are to attain a shared understanding of one another's point of view. As Harriet Lerner notes in her book *The Dance of Anger*, "We cannot make another person change his or her steps to an old dance, but if we change our own steps, the dance no longer can continue in the same predictable pattern."[3] We can have a profound positive impact on our relationships, groups, and organizations if we take responsibility and start focusing on conveying what we really *think* and *feel*, and on understanding what the other person thinks and feels.

In this chapter and the next, I'll offer some guidelines to help you effectively speak up about your differences. These chapters do not provide hard-and-fast rules or even things that are always feasible to do. They are meant more to provide a sense of what you should be striving for and to help start you on a journey toward achieving this goal.

SEEKING MUTUAL UNDERSTANDING

When we have a difference with someone, we have three possible responses. One option is to remain silent. Another is to speak up, talking tough, trying to make our point.[4] A third option is to speak up, but seek mutual understanding.

Sara had been a researcher in the development office at a major national magazine for the past five years. The development office was responsible for raising money for the nonprofit sector of the magazine (the magazine had both for-profit and nonprofit entities). It was also responsible for receiving and acknowledging all gifts that were donated to the organization—

everything from small personal checks to corporate stock options. Sara's daily functions included processing letters and gifts from donors. Several letters or packages came in every day. Sara was supposed to open and record each package, enter donor information into the computer database, and then let her coworkers know of the gifts so they could write acknowledgments and follow up with individual donors.

The only problem was that Sara was often slow and sloppy with her work and didn't seem to realize that it mattered. Yet when Sara was slow opening the mail or entering gift information into the computer, the person in charge of accounts didn't have an accurate idea of the money coming into the department, and the person writing thank-you notes couldn't write them in a timely manner. Sara had also been known to enter insufficient address information, making it impossible for a coworker to follow up with an acknowledgment letter.

Sara's boss, Michael, had recently joined the organization, and he quickly learned of his staff's frustrations with Sara. Michael knew that he could either remain silent and wait to see how things unfolded, or he could speak with her. But if he were to speak with her, what would he say? Giving performance feedback to a poor performer is one of the toughest things that a manager has to do. Yet if Michael remained silent, he would likely find himself caught in the silent spiral, with profound negative consequences on his relationship with Sara and on her work. And given the pervasive discontent in the office, being silent would also likely have negative ripple effects on his relationships with the other members of his staff.

Let's compare two possible scenarios, both where Michael speaks up—one in which Michael talks tough to Sara and a second in which he seeks mutual understanding with her.

Scenario 1: Talking Tough

Michael calls Sara into his office in front of the rest of the department, making it clear to everyone that he is singling her out. She begrudgingly gets up and heads into his office. He closes the door behind her.

Anxious about what is to follow, Michael immediately launches into a diatribe. "Sara, I'm new here. I have been hearing endless complaints about your lack of engagement in the work. You're holding people up, making it impossible to get our thank-you notes out on time, and when they do go out they are misaddressed and often sloppy. Your peers are disgruntled with your contribution. I cannot have one person ruin it for everyone."

Sara tries to break in and explain herself, but Michael is so determined to make himself heard that he does not acknowledge her attempt. Rather, he continues, "You need to start paying more attention. We cannot have all these mistakes. We cannot be so sloppy in this organization. You know how important our donors are to us. We need to treat them with respect. I cannot keep you here if you don't get your act together."

Michael stops. The room is silent.

Sara, who has been looking down the whole time, suddenly looks up, stares directly at Michael, and firmly states, "We have been incredibly busy with the Christmas season. I am doing the best I can. The donors are still all getting their letters. Don't blame me for all your worries about the department."

Michael, caught off-guard by Sara's hostility, immediately backs off. "Clearly, I don't yet understand the inner workings of the department. I definitely need to look into the issue further." Following a helpless sigh, he adds, "I just hope we can all do the best job possible and make this department a success."

Sara, raising her eyebrows in dismay, mutters, "I think we are doing fine." Then she asks, "Is that all we need to talk about?"

Clearly, this kind of conversation is not constructive. It was never made clear to Sara what was to be the purpose of the meeting. Rather, from the start, she was put on the defensive, being attacked for her behavior. Even worse, Michael took no responsibility for the accusations he put forth, instead attributing them to his staff. And Sara was given no chance to explain herself; Michael never stopped to inquire why she was acting as she was or what they might do about it. Rather, prior to the meeting, he had already jumped to the conclusion that Sara was at fault and that she needed to change. He made no attempt to challenge or verify his assumption. And in the end, nothing was accomplished. Sara was left unaware of the extent to which she was creating problems, and Michael remained unaware of why there was a problem or what might be done to improve the situation.

When we talk tough, as Michael did with Sara, we focus on declaring our own position without fully exploring it or listening to and seeking to understand the other person's perspective. To speak up effectively, in contrast, requires that we take a proactive approach in which we seek to understand the other person's perspective and the reasons behind it. It is not enough to understand that a difference exists. We need to focus on knowing and conveying our thoughts and feelings as well as on facilitating other people's sharing of their thoughts and feelings.

Imagine a very different scenario between Michael and Sara, in which they more successfully seek mutual understanding.

Scenario 2: Seeking Mutual Understanding

Michael walks over to Sara's desk and asks if there might be a convenient time for them to briefly discuss her role in the department. They agree to meet later that afternoon in a conference room on a different floor in the building. When Sara and

Michael get together, he starts the conversation by thanking her for meeting with him and telling her his purpose.

Michael says, "I am hoping to discuss the role you've been playing on the team and how you think you've been contributing. I know it's been very busy with the Christmas season. How do you feel things are going?"

Sara responds, "Everything is fine, but I'm not sure why we're meeting."

Michael tries to explain: "It's my sense there's been an increased amount of confusion recently, and we're losing track of some of our key donations. Would you agree?"

Sara answers, "Well, we've had more work recently, so we haven't been able to keep track with the level of detail we once did, but I don't think it's a big deal. We're still getting letters out to all our donors in a reasonable time frame."

Michael, paraphrasing and questioning what he has just heard: "So you don't see it as important to get the letters out more quickly?" Sara nods. Michael then continues, "I'm worried about the time frame. I don't think we can let these things wait so long. I'm also worried that some of these letters are slipping through the cracks. Sara, I really need you to pay more attention to all the details. I'm eager to find a way to help. What can I do?"

Sara, still not convinced there is a problem, asks, "Why are you making such a big deal about this? I don't understand the problem."

Michael tries to explain: "I really think it is important that your work is done well. You have a central job in our group. It's critical that we show the donors respect. When they receive a letter that's late or inaccurate or crumpled, it doesn't convey how much their donation matters to us. What you do here is important. Your work is central to the successful functioning of our group."

Sara, surprised, exclaims, "I never really thought about it

that way. I've always felt like I had a mindless job that added little value."

Suddenly realizing how Sara has been feeling, Michael wonders aloud, "Do you think there are ways we could make your job more exciting? How about we brainstorm some possibilities?" After creating a list of ideas, they agree to each go off and think some more about Sara's job, and to reconvene the following week.

ॐ

From the start, this second scenario got off in a more constructive direction. Instead of embarrassing Sara and making it clear that she was being called into the boss's office, Michael set a mutually convenient time at a location where others in the department would not be aware the meeting was occurring. Michael further made sure to state his purpose at the start of the meeting. And he made an effort to engage Sara in the discussion, trying to understand her point of view and the reasons behind it. Rather than make assumptions about what was at the source of her behavior, he asked her open-ended questions—questions that gave her broad latitude in how to answer.[5] He also paraphrased Sara's responses—saying back to her in his own words what he heard her saying—to ensure that he really understood her. Michael also tried to convey his point of view and what was at the source of his concerns. And he communicated an open and accepting climate, expressing a desire to work with Sara to make the necessary changes.[6]

When seeking understanding of other people's thoughts and feelings, it's critical to start with the data. What are the "facts" of the matter? We know how we feel. We know what we think. We know why we feel and think these things. We know what has happened and what should happen—from *our* perspective. We also know the behavior we have observed in other people. We know what they have said and how they have acted. All of that is data we can bring to the discussion. What we *don't* know is how others think or feel, why they behaved as they did, or why they said what they said. That is data that only the other person can bring to the discussion. Our job is to share the data as we know them and to ask questions of others to understand the data as they know them.[7]

In scenario 1, Michael jumped to conclusions about Sara's behavior. He made no attempt to understand what was at the source of her behavior—why she was behaving as she was. In contrast, in scenario 2, Michael got to the heart of the matter— the data; as a result, he learned that Sara felt her work was mindless and of little value.

One component of surfacing the key data is our willingness and ability to share what we know and feel. Equally important is being able to gather data from other people effectively. This requires listening to understand other people's perspectives— asking open-ended questions and paraphrasing back their comments. It involves being able to hear what they say and respond in ways that further encourage them to continue to share their thoughts and feelings. When we don't like what they are saying, we may be tempted to try to shut them down. We may be tempted to interrupt and insert our own opinions, make excuses, or start blaming. But we need to hold ourselves back and give other people the space to share their thoughts and feelings. Moreover, we need to be empathetic—trying to put ourselves in their place and understand their perspectives.

If, however, we only ask questions and listen to other people's perspectives, we will better understand their points of view, but they won't better understand ours. We need to learn more about others' views, but they also need to learn more about ours. We need to effectively balance speaking up with understanding what other people have to say.[8]

It may be the case that even after differences are effectively expressed and mutual understanding is achieved, consensus about a solution or course of action still cannot be reached. Sara's performance, for instance, might not have improved, and Michael might eventually have had to fire her. But at least by having a constructive conversation, Sara would receive the feedback she needed in a way that was most likely to enable her to make the necessary improvements.

In other situations, the difference will not revolve around a person's performance but might revolve around a decision. And having sought to understand each other, we may still find ourselves stuck at an impasse. When it becomes clear that everyone understands one another's point of view and the reasons behind it, yet no solution or consensus is in sight, it may be necessary to draw the line and move on. Enormous amounts of time can be wasted and productivity severely hindered if too much time and energy are spent trying to resolve conflicts beyond the point of mutual understanding. To move forward and not dwell on differences, someone—having benefited from understanding the conflicting viewpoints—may, in the end, need to make a unilateral decision. But if the exchange has been effective, the decision is now being made by a person informed of the differences that do exist. While some people may not agree with the decision, at least everyone should understand the reasoning behind it.

The story of Herman Miller, the renowned furniture company, shows what can happen when people speak up but no one makes a final decision about how to proceed. As William Isaacs describes in his article "The Perils of Shared Ideals":

> *In the early 1990s, [Herman Miller] struggled and lost considerable strategic momentum because of the fallout from its own cherished "participative" ideal. . . . Artisans and designers argued that the company needed to return to its roots of design leadership. Other voices insisted that the*

key to the future lay in improving business and marketing operations. Over the next few years, as the company followed both directions, tensions grew deeper. There were endless abstract conversations about the company's management philosophy, but little agreement about setting immediate priorities. Nor did anyone talk about their factionalism. They couldn't talk about it—because the ideal of participation made it almost impossible to see that they were factionalized. After all, "everyone had a voice." But the company lacked any way to translate that voice into action.[9]

The key is that speaking up effectively means that everyone has a voice and everyone listens to everyone else's voice. It does not, however, mean that people always gets their way or agree on what happens in the end. It only means that each person's voice is heard and understood so that an informed decision can be made.

TURNING THE SITUATION AROUND

To achieve mutual understanding we may first need to turn the situation around.[10] If we have been silenced by another—whether by suppressing or by glossing—we must first find a way to draw attention to the fact that our difference has not been effectively addressed. Then, once we reopen the conversation about our difference, we will further need to approach it more effectively, seeking mutual understanding.

The support staff at a preeminent law firm was broken down into departments (e.g., library, legal assistance, information technology, proofreading, secretarial). Each department had a representative who served as department head and was responsible for expressing the interests of the rest of the members of the department. Linda was head of the library. Robert was the manager of operations, responsible for overseeing the support staff and for working closely with the department heads. He also was a lawyer by training and a partner in the firm.

Linda went to Robert to complain about the evaluation process for the support staff. Robert and the other lawyers in the firm would critique the support staff when it came time for salary reviews. Linda felt that many of the lawyers weren't fair in their evaluations. They were irascible and aloof, she argued. It was not right that they had the power to determine raises and promotions. Robert, however, vehemently disagreed. He told Linda to think of the lawyers as if they were clients for whom each department was providing a service. If a lawyer needed something proofread, he'd go to the proofreading department and employ the services of a reader. If he needed a legal document, he'd go to the librarians. "If you think of the lawyers as your clients," Robert explained, "you can see why they have every expectation to be able to critique the quality of service." When Linda pressed again, Robert got fed up and said, "This is the way we do it around here, and this is the way it's going to continue!"

Linda was stunned. She said nothing more and quietly left. Robert assumed that because his viewpoint was a "no-brainer," the issue would go away.

Linda was in a particularly difficult situation. Having been suppressed, to speak up further she would need to reopen the conversation and turn the situation around. Let's imagine two possible scenarios, one in which Linda says nothing more to Robert and a second in which Linda manages to effectively turn the situation around.

Scenario 1: Keeping Quiet

Linda never again raises the topic with Robert, nor does she ever bring it up in a department meeting. However, she complains about the situation with other department heads behind Robert's back. As news of Robert's insensitivity spreads throughout the support staff, it becomes viewed as a "management doesn't listen" attitude.

꒳

Clearly, in this scenario, Linda did not take responsibility for the situation. Instead, she turned to others and blamed Robert. In turning to others, she could have built a coalition to enable her to confront Robert and the other partners constructively. But rather, she turned to others to gossip, spreading the discontent and finger-pointing.

Now compare that scenario with the following, more constructive, one.

Scenario 2: Seeking Mutual Understanding

After her initial conversation with Robert, Linda takes some time to calm down and figure out how to proceed. She realizes that Robert has tried to suppress her. However, she also recognizes that she has not done an adequate job of explaining herself to him. She believes her point of view is reasonable but knows she needs to find a way to better communicate it.

During the following week, Linda reviews the previous year's performance evaluations and notes the obvious discrepancies between what is in the evaluations and her own perceptions of each person's performance. She also talks with various staff members to gather some concrete examples of their experiences with the evaluation process. She finds that in many evaluations, people received negative critiques that were very general and had no supporting evidence. Even when there were specifics or concrete examples, these were often incorrect in some way.

Feeling confident that she has collected enough data to build her case, Linda sets up another meeting with Robert.

Linda starts this meeting by saying, "I know that you don't think the issue with the performance evaluation process is important. But it is very important to the staff, and we would like you to understand our point of view. I don't feel comfortable dropping the issue as you suggested. I would like a chance to better explain my perspective."

Linda then tells Robert that some of her best people are getting poor reviews. She describes the problems she has uncovered—such as frequent lack of evidence and sometimes outright errors in supporting critiques—and presents some examples, making them as detailed as possible without revealing anyone's specific identity. Linda further tells Robert, "I am concerned that our best staff are going to leave. It is that big of a deal to them. We need to try to find some solution, or the firm is going to suffer."

Hearing the genuine concern in Linda's tone and impressed with the data she has collected, Robert thanks her for bringing the issue up again. He still thinks that the lawyers' input is important for the support staff to hear but agrees that perhaps the process needs to be rethought.

Robert and Linda decide to explore the issue further. Linda agrees to continue talking to staff members about their experiences and to write up a report. Robert agrees to talk to some of the lawyers about how they view the process and the effort they put into it. They decide to meet in a couple of weeks to discuss what they have each learned.

࿋

In scenario 2, Linda took some important steps to turn the situation around. First, she took some time out to calm down and think about what to do. When she met with Robert, she let him know that she was aware that he wanted to drop the issue but that she wasn't yet ready to do so. By bringing up their difference again, she made it clear to Robert that she couldn't be silenced so easily. Also, by doing some research before raising the issue again, Linda was able to focus the discussion on the data. And, as a result, she was able to get Robert to appreciate that she had a valid perspective that needed further consideration.

ACTING DEVIANT

In addition to turning the situation around, seeking mutual understanding often requires challenging deeply entrenched patterns. Norms become established. And as the silent spiral spins, it feels increasingly risky to speak up and break these norms.

A product development team designing a color copier at a high-tech organization had a norm that at their weekly status meeting everyone would provide an update on their progress, but no one would ask any follow-up questions or provide any suggestions. So problems would often be reported, but no discussion would ensue about how to address them. Time after time, this norm inhibited people from speaking up.

One day, Jay, the engineering representative on the team, reported to the rest of the members, "The technical glitch we are currently having with the paper feeder is probably going to delay us close to two weeks." Normally, no one would have said anything in response. If one of the team members had an issue with what happened during the meeting, he might tell their boss, the team's manager, but only outside of the meeting when the manager could decide privately how he wanted to address the issue. On this day, however, in the meeting, Tom, the marketing representative, expressed his concern about the delay, thus breaking the norm of silence.

As Tom spoke up, he worried about the consequences. He worried what his boss—who was sitting at the head of the table—would think. He worried what his peers would think. It was taboo to speak. However, Tom had had an inkling that this slip in the schedule might be coming, and he had carefully calculated just how costly it would be for the product and ultimately the company. Still, he knew that speaking up at this moment could negatively affect how people on the team perceived him.

If Tom spoke up, talking tough, his worst fears about speaking up might indeed have come true. A scenario like the following might have ensued.

Scenario 1: Talking Tough

Tom, unable to hold back, attacks Jay: "You guys in engineering are going to cost us the launch date. We won't be first to market. Why do you always do this to us? Don't you realize you're going to ruin the product's potential in the market?"

Jay attacks back: "You in marketing always want us to launch products that aren't yet finished. They still have bugs in them. We look terrible. The company looks terrible. Our customers get mad. It makes no sense. We need to fix the problems before we launch the product. We have no choice."

At this point, a few other people try to silence Tom so as to enable the meeting to move on. Tom, however, continues to argue that a delay will be costly. No one seems to agree. Finally Tom drops the topic. Afterward he feels that team members who used to respect him are suddenly pointing fingers. When he passes them in the hallway, he frequently hears them whispering, but they shut up as soon as they see him.

༃

Compare that scenario with the following one, in which Tom seeks mutual understanding with Jay.

Scenario 2: Seeking Mutual Understanding

Hearing the news that the launch will be delayed, Tom says to Jay: "I understand it's critical from your perspective to delay the product and fix the problem with the paper feeder, but can you help me to understand what will be lacking if we opt to ignore this fix?" Tom further notes, "I think we need to weigh the costs and benefits because the cost of a two-week delay will be enormous from a marketing perspective. We almost certainly won't be first to market. I think we need to be convinced that the benefits of fixing the problem outweigh the costs of slipping our launch date and losing first-to-market status. I'm not convinced as to which way to go. I think we each need to provide more information so we can collectively make the most informed decision."

Jay then responds with similar openness: "I think having a fully functioning product is essential—as you well know. But I also understand that being first to market matters. If this slip in the schedule will make the difference, we could put in place a short-term, work-around solution to the paper feeder problem. This is certainly not ideal. It will take extra time because we will need to go back and fix the problem in addition to creating this short-term fix. However, given the issue of being first to market, maybe it is worth it?"

᠀

In scenario 2, by clearly conveying his own concerns but also asking about Jay's issues, Tom successfully opened up a discussion of what was at stake for both sides. Hearing the profound cost of a slip in schedule for the product, Jay felt comfortable engaging in a collaborative discussion about their options. The more each shared, the more comfortable the other felt sharing his concerns, and the more they each came to understand the issue from the other's perspective.

Although fear usually prevents us from doing as Tom did—speaking up in the face of a norm of silence—the consequences often are not nearly as dreadful as we fantasize. Indeed, people who challenge the established order, and do so constructively, often end up demonstrating that there are other acceptable ways of acting that do not have the feared consequences.[11] By opening up a constructive conversation, Tom not only succeeded in having the conversation about the launch date that he felt was so necessary, he further showed others on the team the very real possibility that their norm of keeping quiet after each status report was indeed not only breakable but that breaking it could be desirable. In the end, breaking a norm—by seeking understanding, as opposed to talking tough—raises questions about the very purpose and legitimacy of the norm itself.[12]

We don't have to make huge breaches to be successful; we can simply start to be ourselves and challenge norms of silence in small, steady ways. Over time these incremental adjustments can have a powerful effect. Small wins can eventually add up to a big change.[13]

Actions have ripple effects. Others will be inspired by the changes. Just one person acting in a way that is atypical can have an effect on the larger system and culture. For one thing, it makes it easier for others to act in similar ways. When someone goes first, it helps others feel that it is okay to express their differences. In many cases, others may be thinking and feeling the same way but are choosing to hide their true thoughts and feelings. Take the Hans Christian Andersen fairy tale "The Emperor's New Clothes." No one dared tell the emperor he was wearing no clothes until a young child cried out, "But he doesn't have anything on!" As the story goes, only then "The people whispered among each other and repeated what the child had said. . . . 'He has nothing on!' Shouted all the people at last."[14]

Remember the Abilene Paradox in Chapter 4? No one in the family wanted to go to Abilene, but everyone agreed to go because they all thought that's what everyone else wanted to do. If any one family member had spoken up, others would likely have admitted their true preferences as well. When one person speaks up, others are likely to come out of the woodwork, and soon the one turns into many—generating even more power.

Even if others are not moved to express their differences about the same issue, the act of voicing ourselves can inspire others to voice their own thoughts, beliefs, or feelings about other issues. When people see no one else breaking norms of silence, they believe that doing so is too risky. However, when one person violates a norm of silence, others view it as a signal that it is okay for them to do the same.

Still, to achieve even small wins is not easy, and we should not underestimate the fear speaking up can arouse or the consequences that can result. However, deviating from a norm need not be associated with dysfunctionality. Deviance represents variety. It is a creative act. It's an act of searching out and inventing new ways of doing things. It can point out needed change and provide a glimpse of a new world. It can lead to something beneficial. Resisting and challenging existing norms provides alternatives. Without people violating norms, the world would be a boring, stale, drab place to live.[15]

SOME POINTS OF CLARIFICATION

Effectively expressing difference means ensuring that we convey our thoughts and feelings in a way that other people can understand while also making a concerted effort to understand where others are coming from and why. Effectively expressing difference, however, does not mean expressing every difference. The goal is to ensure mutual understanding on core issues in important relationships.

We need to figure out which issues matter to us.[16] Some issues are simply not worth raising—they just don't matter enough, or they are not core to our relationship or our work. We don't want to waste time and effort getting bogged down trying to deal with these issues. To just let something go can be an act of maturity.

We must make sure, though, to speak up about the issues that matter to us and to our work. Most people tend to err on the side of excess caution and not speaking up enough rather than speaking up too much. Our goal should be to shift from asking ourselves whether this is one of those rare times that we should speak up to instead asking ourselves whether this is one of those rare times we should remain quiet.

If there were some hard-and-fast rules about when to raise issues and when to leave them alone, at least knowing when we had to speak up would be made easy. However, because situations are always different and because our relationships with those involved vary as well, there are no simple rules. Whether to raise an issue can be decided only on the basis of the specific situation and the specific people involved.

Sometimes the timing is not right. For instance, when emotions are highly charged, it is important to wait until everyone involved has had a chance to cool down. We want to speak when we can present a clear explanation of our perspective without venting or blaming, when we can focus on hearing and understanding where the other person is coming from, and when we perceive that the other person is in a position to do the same with us.

When facing an impending deadline, we often have to make a difficult choice about when to speak about a difference. Sometimes speaking up may not only slow us down, but it will be of little value for the immediate task at hand. And sometimes, even if at the moment speaking up would be of value, we still don't have the time.

On some occasions we may decide the timing is not right to speak up. We may decide to wait until some deadline or some other self-appointed time passes. But it is critical that we not wait indefinitely. A little fable about a farmer with a wagon full of apples helps to illustrate the reason. The farmer stopped a man on the side of the road and asked, "How far is it to market?" The man on the side of the road responded, "It is an hour away, if you go slow." He continued, "If you go fast, it will take you all day." Why? Because there was a bump in the road up ahead, and if the farmer tried to go too fast, he would hit the bump, his apples would fall out all over, and he would have to spend all day picking up the apples.

For important issues that are open to different interpretations or reactions, making sure to engage in a discussion of them at some point is critical. If we don't make this time, these issues, as well as the underlying resentment caused by not addressing them, can cause much greater problems later. With each act of silencing, the difficulty of speaking up next time only grows and so too do the costs of staying quiet.

Of course, sometimes we'll find ourselves in difficult situations that make all this good advice about effectively expressing difference hard to implement. Such constraints as reward systems, authority structures, who we are, and who the other person is can make speaking up very difficult. Sometimes, too, no matter what we say or do we cannot improve the situation. In these instances we may have some painful choices to make: Do we choose to stay in the particular relationship or situation regardless? Do we choose to leave? These are not easy questions to answer or even to think about. We may decide to stay in the relationship but reduce our expectations. Or we may decide it is not worth it.

Sometimes, it really is the other person or the situation, and there is nothing that we can do about it. All too often, though, we attribute our differences to something beyond our control even though they are not. As a result we end up letting our relationships, and in turn a part of our organization, die unnecessarily.

CHAPTER ELEVEN

Finding Support and Supporting Others

To effectively express differences, we need to turn situations around, break norms, and find ways to convey our thoughts and feelings while also enabling others to convey their thoughts and feelings. There is no getting around these demands. However, there are ways to ease the stress associated with speaking up. As employees, we can gain support from talking to other people or from forming coalitions with others. People in positions of authority can also help their subordinates to feel safe in speaking up. A leader can role-model the desired behavior and create and reinforce conditions that enable others to feel comfortable in expressing their differences.

FINDING SUPPORT FROM OTHERS

Sometimes we get caught up in our differences and cannot see a way out. A colleague, friend, or family member may be able to help. Indeed, anyone whom we trust and respect may be of help. They can act as a sounding board and challenge our assumptions. They can also provide support and help us to think through how we might proceed.

When turning to others for help and support, we need to be careful not to complain or otherwise talk negatively about the person with whom we differ. Gossiping with someone else only provides a temporary release of the negative emotions that result from silencing conflict. Rather than helping to cure the underlying problem, gossip only fuels the unhealthy dynamic. We must, instead, approach a conversation with a third party with an open mind, asking for their help in thinking through a situation. In doing so, we force ourselves to think about how to approach the situation constructively, and we will likely gain a partner in the process, someone who can help us reflect on what to say and do.

We need to make sure to find someone who will stay neutral and be honest with us. It doesn't help to talk to a third party who just agrees with whatever we say or reinforces our desire to blame the other person. What can greatly benefit us, though, is help and support in our efforts to explain our point of view and to seek to understand the other person's point of view.

In addition to getting support from the sidelines, we may also find support among people who are experiencing the same or similar issues. When we reveal our own thoughts, we may find that others want to join our cause. Nancy Hopkins, a scientist at the Massachusetts Institute of Technology (MIT), believed that gender discrimination was impeding her research and putting unnecessary obstacles in her path.[1] Over and over, she found herself having to fight much harder than her male colleagues for such resources as lab space.

At first, Hopkins explained away each incident. But after years of dealing with the same issues, she could not take it any longer. Reaching this point was very difficult for Hopkins. As she describes it: "For several days, I was paralyzed. But then, happily, despair turned to anger. I decided I would try to solve my problems, try to change my working environment."[2] She drafted a letter to the administration. But a male friend of hers, after reading the letter, questioned, "You're not planning to send that, are you?"[3]

Still determined to send the letter, Hopkins decided to show it to a female colleague whom she regarded as politically savvy. Recalling the incident, Hopkins describes how nervous she felt about showing her colleague the letter. Hopkins feared she was the only woman who suffered from these kinds of difficulties, and she worried that if she was really such a good scientist, she would not be caught up in these issues.

Hopkins anxiously awaited the other woman's reaction. As the woman read the letter, she was quiet and serious at first. Then, to Hopkins's surprise, the woman said, "I'd like to sign this letter, and I think we should go and see the president. I've believed for a long time that tenured women faculty here are not treated equally."[4] It turned out that she too had witnessed the biases Hopkins described but had also thought she was alone in her perception. Hopkins was speechless.

The two women reasoned that if they agreed that discrimination existed in their workplace, other female colleagues might agree as well. They decided to talk to the fifteen other tenured women faculty in the School of Science at MIT. Again Hopkins felt embarrassed to bring up the issue with the next woman, but this woman too immediately asked, "Do you have anything I could sign?"[5] By the end of the first day, ten women had agreed to sign the letter. In the end, fourteen of the fifteen women they approached decided to join the initiative. According to Hopkins, for many of these women, it wasn't an easy thing to do. She explains, "To take this step was hard—embarrassing and awkward. The women wanted to operate as quietly as possible. We wanted to fix things and just go back to our labs and classrooms."[6]

The women decided to send a joint letter to the dean of science that stated: "We believe that unequal treatment of women who come to MIT makes it more difficult for them to succeed, causes them to be accorded less recognition when they do, and contributes so substantially to a poor quality of life that these women can actually become negative role models for younger women."[7] The letter further asked the dean to establish a committee to collect data and investigate whether women really were unfairly treated with respect to resources and compensation.

After sending the letter, Hopkins and the other women met with the dean in person. Hopkins recalls that the meeting with the dean "was a very tense moment."[8] Fortunately, he was supportive and wanted to look into the matter. Other administrators, however, were less supportive. But with the backing of the president, the dean moved forward and established a committee that included a tenured woman from each department and three men who were or had been heads of their departments.

Over the next two years, the committee learned that what had been attributed over and over to individual circumstances was actually a pattern of discrimination. It was only when the women across different departments got together and presented their collective concerns, however, that these patterns of inequities became evident. As a result, several changes were made at MIT to try to ensure gender equity. It took a group of women, many of whom the dean knew to be excellent scientists, sitting in his office and all telling the same story that convinced him that there was something seriously wrong.[9]

Don't underestimate the potential of multiple voices as a way to overcome a lack of formal authority. Don't overlook the power of the collective. Mobilizing other people to support a cause can be a potent way to create change.[10] A coalition has the advantages of more legitimacy, resources, and power. It also helps in providing support to one another, as it is easier to speak up when we know we aren't alone. Building coalitions can sometimes seem threatening since we don't always know how other people are going to respond to what we want to say or do. But we may be surprised to find that more people agree with us than we had thought—they too were just unsure what to do and didn't know others were concerned as well.

CREATING CHANGE FROM POSITIONS OF AUTHORITY

If you are in a position of authority, you have even more power to trigger far-reaching change in the norms of silence governing behavior in your group or organization. I should be clear that I am not advocating that having conflict is necessarily better than not having conflict; rather, I am advocating that if you are in a position of authority you try to establish an environment in which people feel comfortable expressing the conflicts that they do have.

After climbing the ranks in a management consulting firm, Bill had recently been elected a junior partner. His project team included himself and eight consultants. Bill was responsible for the day-to-day project management and client relationship, while Martin—a senior partner and Bill's mentor—provided guidance to Bill and gave the final approval on the work for the client.

The team quickly found itself needing to work extraordinarily long hours—even more than was typical for their consulting firm, which was known for having long work hours. Bill himself felt overwhelmed with the work. He had always been disorganized but had managed to get things done. Now he worried that things were getting out of control. But at least, he reassured himself, no one on the team had complained.

After a couple of months, however, Martin approached Bill and told him that he had been hearing rumors from other partners that Bill's project had become a "death march"—a label consultants at the firm applied to particularly difficult projects, especially those in which no one got any sleep. Martin cautioned Bill that such problems on the project would hurt his career trajectory, as good consultants wouldn't want to work for him anymore—and getting good consultants to work on his projects was essential for his career success. Martin advised Bill to find a way to turn things around before the project ended.

Upon hearing this news, Bill felt devastated. This was his first project as a junior partner, and he desperately wanted to do a good job. He worried about how the consultants on the team saw him as a manager and feared that they blamed him for the problems. He was concerned that he now had a bad reputation and that no one would want to work for him again. He felt annoyed that no one on his team had said anything to him directly and instead were talking to others behind his back. Nonetheless, he knew he had to do something.

Bill decided he should talk to his team directly and hear from them what was wrong and what they might do differently. He felt nervous about doing so. He was afraid of undermining his authority as their leader, but he reasoned that he didn't have much choice.

His team was supposed to work at the client's office each Monday through Thursday, returning to their own firm's office on Fridays. However, they rarely followed this schedule because of their workload. Instead, they tended to work Monday through Friday at the client's office and then in their own firm's office over the weekends. But Bill decided to make an exception—he thought that for them to be able to talk openly about the project and their feelings related to it, it would be better for them to get together at their own office, away from the client. He worried about their taking time off from the project, but he knew that this was an important discussion to have.

Bill scheduled a conference room at their firm's office for the following Friday. He sent an e-mail message to everyone on his team, letting them know about the meeting. He followed up the message by personally talking to each team member to explain what the meeting was about. He told each of them, "I realize this has been a tough project so far, and I want to make it the best experience for you possible. I'd like for us all to talk openly about our perceptions of how things are going and what improvements we can make for the remainder of it. I hope you'll think a little bit about what could be done differently in preparation for our meeting on Friday."

When the meeting itself began on Friday morning, Bill started off by saying to the team, with great passion in his voice, "I wanted us all to meet together today so that we can talk about how the project is going and what improvements can be made. I know we've all been working extremely long hours, and that it has been tough on each of you personally. As you know, this is my first project to manage as a partner. I want this experience to be good for all of you—and for our work to benefit our client. I need your help to make it that way. I'm hoping we can think together about how to improve the situation. What can we change to make it so we get the work done to the best of our ability but don't have to kill ourselves in the process?"

Bill felt nervous—he had laid himself on the line with his team and hoped that they would respond positively. At first, no one said a word. After a long pause, one of the men on the team spoke about the trouble he was having at home—his wife was constantly upset because she never saw him. Two other men—who both had spouses and children—said it had been tough on their families as well, and that they felt things needed to change. Bill was single and had no family responsibilities, but he did his best to show his concern for what they were saying. He felt terrible about the toll the project was taking on everyone's personal lives and he told them so. The team spent a couple of hours talking about the difficulties of balancing the demands of a consulting job with their personal and family responsibilities. Everyone seemed to be struggling with this.

During the lunch break, Bill thought about next steps. They were going to have to make some changes so that the project didn't consume so much of people's time, but he didn't know how to do this and still deliver a quality result to the client. To him, the amount of time spent working had always equaled good results—but perhaps there was a different way.

When they got back together after lunch, Bill suggested that they shift from talking about the problems they were facing to brainstorming about potential solutions. He told them that it would be helpful to set some ground rules for the discussion. They listed on the whiteboard a set of rules, including be open and honest; take personal risks; listen to one another before responding; tolerate one another's differences; ask questions to help clarify; support others. During the rest of the afternoon, using these ground rules as a set of guidelines, the team talked about what could be done differently. The discussion was sometimes painful for Bill, but he stuck with it and tried not to get defensive. The team members told Bill that one of the big reasons why they had to work such long hours was that they didn't get timely feedback from him. They had two deadlines each week—a report for the client that they delivered every Friday and a preliminary version of the report that they gave to the senior partner, Martin, on Wednesdays. The team shared with Bill that they had a hard time getting his attention and feedback on these reports until late in the evening before they were due, and then they'd have to stay working into the night to respond to his comments. If he would give them feedback earlier in the day, they wouldn't waste so much time going in a different direction from what he wanted.

This seemed like a good place to start. Together they created a schedule in which Bill would meet with each member of the team on Tuesday and Thursday mornings to go over their work. They agreed to give it a try and then have a follow-up meeting in a month to review how things were going. Perhaps at that time, they would think of other changes they could make as well.

Although it had been difficult to hear the feedback from the team on his management style, Bill felt that the day had been extremely valuable. Most of all, he was relieved that his team had responded so well to his invitation to speak up. And he hoped that, in the future, when his team members had an issue, they would feel more comfortable in bringing it up.

Bill effectively modeled the behavior he wanted others to exhibit. He was open and honest. He made himself vulnerable. Just like everyone else in the group, as a leader, one must live the change one wants others to make, exhibiting the desired openness. Leaders have to be willing to ask questions, show genuine interest, and make themselves understood.

Leaders have a deeply ingrained sense that they are supposed to know what is going on and that it is simply unacceptable for them to act as if they do not know. Indeed, part of the image of being a successful leader is putting on "an air of confident knowledge."[11] To say "I don't know" is to go against the norms of what a leader is expected to say. Bill, however, found the courage to ask for help. In doing so, he opened up a conversation with his team.

Bill also successfully used his power to create an environment in which other people began to feel safe in expressing their differences. Leaders have an opportunity to create safe space— to create a "container"—in which people feel more secure in taking risks. The hope is that once people open up with one another and have a positive experience under these conditions, they will be more likely to bring this new behavior into their everyday work and begin to change their patterns. The more people speak up and find a positive response, the less risky they will perceive speaking up to be, and the more likely they and others will be to speak up about differences in the future.

Leaders can signal their intention to create safe space as Bill did, by labeling a meeting as such, by gathering in a distinct location, by establishing ground rules, and by being clear at the start about the purpose of the meeting. They must also follow through. People need to see that they are not punished for revealing mistakes, that there is a willingness to share responsibility, and that there is genuine curiosity to learn how everyone can do better in the future.

Harry was a battalion commander, charged with training and leading over five hundred combat soldiers. His unit had just completed a mock battle against a highly trained opposing unit at the National Training Center. The exercise ended with a review of the battle. Statistics were reported, including how many had died, how many were wounded, and how much equipment was destroyed. The natural reaction after such statistics are announced is for the losing unit to debate the numbers, claiming that the results overestimate the casualties and that the unit has not been defeated as badly as the statistics make it seem. But Harry wanted none of that. He knew that his soldiers had been unquestionably defeated and that the defeat reflected poorly on him and his battalion. His unit was getting evaluated on this exercise, and they had failed miserably. He knew that there was no hiding from that reality. Despite his battalion's best efforts, the enemy had somehow managed to surprise them and gain the advantage with incredible speed. It was not clear how that was possible. Was there a technical failure with the equipment? Had the electronic sensors failed? Were the unit's scouts and early warning devices poorly positioned? How could this have happened?

In the debriefing immediately following the battle, Harry stood up in front of his entire unit and announced, "If this had been a real battle, two-thirds of us would be dead." He continued, "I was at fault. I failed you." He explained that he had failed to send in the reserves in a timely manner. At a critical point in the battle, he had received an intelligence report indicating that the enemy had somehow breached his security forces and was quickly advancing deep into friendly lines. Harry was in such disbelief that the enemy could have surprised them and that his reserves could be so badly needed so quickly that he simply did not trust the information. And so he hesitated. Ultimately, his indecision cost them the battle. He stood before his men and took responsibility for their failure.

At first, no one said a word. Then, Nick, a very junior enlisted soldier in the battalion slowly stood up. With his head bowed, he said, "No sir, it was not your fault. I fell asleep on duty." A hush came over the group. Nick, as a scout, was to act as the eyes and ears of the battalion commander. Positioned well forward of friendly lines, scouts are responsible for detecting enemy movements and alerting the battalion. Almost for certain, no one would ever have discovered that Nick had fallen asleep on duty had he not admitted it.

Harry was shocked. It was not all the terrible things he had feared about his personal failings—his tactics, his plan, his indecision—but rather the carelessness of one of his men that was making them all look terrible in the eyes of his superiors. This young soldier had failed his duty; he had fallen asleep, perhaps the worst thing that a scout can do on the battlefield.

Rather than focus on Nick's failure, however, Harry quickly redirected the unit's attention toward uncovering the deeper cause of the underlying problem—the exhaustion his men were suffering. Harry was well aware that most of his men had not slept at all in the past three days. He asked Nick directly a few questions: "How long has it been since you slept? How many hours did you sleep?" He then asked the rest of the battalion how many hours they had slept in the past three days. He told them, "Don't put up your hands, but answer to yourself, how many of you slept during the opening rounds of the enemy attack?" Following an uneasy, nervous laughter that spread throughout the soldiers, Harry continued, "Nick is a good soldier. All of you are good soldiers. We need to focus on the bigger issue here: How can we sustain our capabilities during continuous operations in such high-intensity situations?"

The discussion that followed led to profound learning for this battalion. What they learned, however, had nothing to do with the particulars of this attack. Rather, by publicly admitting his own personal failure, this young soldier enabled the analysis of the situation to shift to a much deeper inquiry about the underlying cause of their failure.

Ultimately, Harry had set the tone for this discussion. Had Harry, the most senior leader in the unit, not started by debriefing his own failures, it is highly unlikely that Nick—one of the most junior soldiers in the battalion—would have admitted to falling asleep. Moreover, Harry carefully guided the response Nick received when he did speak up. At this moment, Harry could have attributed the failure of the battle to Nick and framed the ensuing discussion around blame. Instead, Harry quickly shifted the focus of attention from Nick to the larger problem they all faced. And in the end, this unit gained a rich appreciation for the importance of speaking up and admitting one's mistakes.

Leaders need to facilitate the conditions for speaking up. They also need to ensure appropriate responses when people do speak up—to ensure that nothing punitive occurs, especially when what people say could be viewed as problematic. People watch the leader's reaction to determine how mistakes are really treated. If a situation is handled effectively, it encourages people to speak up again next time. The leader's goal should be to create contexts in which people feel comfortable speaking up and are accepted for doing so—and thus come to see the value in doing it. Part of creating such an environment is to ensure that people's raises and promotions are not negatively affected by their openness—especially if they reveal problems or mistakes.[12]

༄

After reading all this good advice for leaders on how to create change in organization norms, don't get discouraged if you are not a senior leader, and definitely don't conclude that there's nothing you can do. The rest of us cannot just sit around and wait for others to change our organizations. Just as blaming someone else will not get us anywhere productive, neither will blaming our leaders. There is no question that some situations could be made easier if senior leaders made certain changes. But we must stop waiting for others to do it for us. Every one of us can and must try to make a difference. When we silence ourselves, we perpetuate norms of silence and become increasingly inclined to silence in the future. If, instead, we start to speak up, we create the potential for new norms to evolve and virtuous rather than vicious spirals to be set in motion.

What Might Have Been . . .

IN NOVEMBER 1999, the members of Versity's top management team met to discuss their vision. They spent the day in a nondescript hotel conference room in Redwood City, California. They were deeply entangled in the silent spiral, and as had become their pattern, again in this meeting, no one effectively expressed their differences. But let's try to imagine what might have happened had someone spoken up.

Imagine the following alternate scenario. Peter starts the day's events by stating: "I've gathered us all together because I believe we have some profound differences about what should be the direction of our company. The founders are a wonderfully competent set of guys who have gotten us to where we are. They have a deep knowledge of our current market, and they bring the only technical skills we have in this company. We need to listen to them and understand where they are coming from and why. At the same time, we've recently been joined by a team of managers with rich management experience, and we need to understand their perspective as well. They've been out in the world for many more years and have significant past experience from which to draw. We are incredibly lucky to have one another and to bring such strong complementary skills and experiences to the question at hand.

"Reflecting on our past two months together, I am afraid I have failed to help us appreciate our different strengths and to identify appropriate roles for each of us. We've been in such a hurry from the day I joined that I failed to have us step back and clarify what we each bring to the company and how we can best work together. Our purpose today is twofold. First, we need to spend some time getting to know each other better and figuring out how to work together most effectively. We further need to figure out how we will go forward—what our vision is for the company. We need to draw from our experiences, understand where each of us is coming from, and collectively create a vision. I recognize this is a huge agenda for one day. We may not get through it all today and that's okay. We will meet again soon. To keep pace with the market demands we're facing we must make the time to address our differences. Otherwise, our greatest strength—our diversity—will destroy us."

Had Peter opened the meeting in this way, he would have exhibited the desired openness and made himself vulnerable. By his example he would have encouraged others to do the same— and they likely would have tried to speak up, tentatively at first, to learn how their words were received. Peter would have needed to support those who did speak up—even if they said things that made him uncomfortable or challenged his way of thinking.

For instance, at one point in the vision meeting, Peter started talking about the key focus of the organization, and Clyde brought up the importance of registered users. Frustrated by the importance that Clyde and the other founders constantly attached to user numbers, Peter snapped, "Clyde, you are talking about strategy and we need to stay on topic." To Clyde it was not at all clear what was meant by "strategy" or "vision," but he instantly became silent.

Imagine what might have happened if, instead, Peter had

responded, "Clyde, can you help us understand why you think registered users matter so much?" Clyde, instead of feeling silenced, might have felt encouraged to open up and explain the reasons behind his point of view. He might have responded, "The only way to be successful in the dot-com world is to acquire users. Currently we are falling behind our goals. I think it is essential that we focus on acquiring as many users as possible, as soon as possible, or we will not be able to raise the money that we desperately need to grow this company."

Hearing Clyde's explanation, Peter might have tried to clarify his own point of view: "I agree with you that acquiring users is essential. However, that said, I am concerned that we have a bigger problem we cannot overlook. Currently we are facing many campuses with disgruntled faculty. So far, every time we've approached administrators on a campus where we have a problem, we've been successful at turning the situation around. However, this is a highly time-intensive and risky strategy for us to pursue. It would be preferable if we could find a way to provide something to faculty that not only appealed to them but encouraged them to bring their students to our website. It is much easier for us to attract one faculty member and get their four hundred students in a large lecture class than it is to find ways to appeal to each of the four hundred students directly. I'm not suggesting we do away with notes. I believe notes are a valuable way to market products to students. I am, however, concerned that we focus on attracting, as opposed to upsetting, faculty in the process. What I've come to recognize is that faculty are not just a potential liability and a source of trouble for us. Faculty provide a potential way for us to access large numbers of students and yet require us to find ways to appeal directly to many fewer people in the process."

In his response, in addition to explaining his own point of view, Peter further might have acknowledged the validity of Clyde's concern for registered users. Peter might have suggested that both of their concerns needed to be considered as part of the Versity vision: "Clyde, I don't disagree with you that registered users matter. We need to increase our numbers. There is no question about that. It matters, however, that we find effective ways to build our user base for the longer term. I am afraid that if we adopt user numbers as our primary goal, we will end up doing so at the expense of finding strategically sound longer-term objectives. We must build our user numbers, but we must pay attention to *how* we do so. We want to be a successful company long into the future, and that requires much more than just a large number of users that make us appear temporarily strong."

Of course, Peter might not have taken the responsibility of setting the group on such a constructive path toward mutual understanding, but someone else could have. Anyone on the management team could have pushed for clarification about the goal of the vision meeting.

Imagine the following scenario. When Peter snapped at him, asserting that a focus on registered users was about strategy not vision, Clyde might have found the courage to break their pattern of glossing over their differences: "Peter, every time I mention registered users, you seem to get upset. I'm confused as to what I've said that is problematic. I thought our goal today was to discuss what is most important to the company. To me, there is nothing more important than registered users. It would be very helpful if we could clarify what we are trying to accomplish in today's session. What do we mean by vision? What is our goal today? If I understood better what we're striving to accomplish, I'd be more able to contribute to the discussion."

Once the group came to some agreement on the goal of the meeting, each time they tried to dismiss something as "not vision and therefore something to be discussed on another day," imagine what might have happened if Clyde had further said, "I'm confused. Can someone help me understand why that does not fit our definition of today's goal? It sounds to me like that really is relevant to what we outlined as today's goal." By pushing the group to clarify their goal and then using that goal as a point of reference to help expose inconsistencies, Clyde would likely have been able to help people recognize the importance and relevance of what was *not* being said.

Whether it was Peter or Clyde or someone else involved who had initiated the shift to a more open stance toward difference, any one of them could have further helped the group explore these differences. If any one of them had tried constructively to facilitate more open communication—conveying his perspective and seeking to ensure that he understood the perspectives of the rest of the management team—others involved would likely have reciprocated.

In the process, the members of the management team would likely have discovered how little they understood about one another's perspectives and how much they were blaming other people for problems that they themselves played a large part in perpetuating. The founders might have learned how their tight grip on the company and their unwillingness to trust the professional managers was undermining the managers' ability to do what they believed to be in the company's best interest. Moreover, the founders might have come to understand not only how they were creating a problem for the professional managers but why the professional managers actually did have an important point of view about the future direction of the company and, in particular, about the potential importance of IZIO. In the process, the founders might also have come to recognize that the professional managers were not nearly as terrible as they had come to view them—as an incompetent, unnecessary layer of bureaucracy that did not care about the company. The founders might, instead, have come to appreciate that the professional managers very much wanted to find ways to enable a successful future for the company, but to do so required that they all be more tolerant of uncertainty and accepting of experimentation.

The professional managers might also have gained some important insight into both themselves and the founders. The professional managers might have come to realize that they had failed to effectively explain to the founders what they perceived to be the profound problems that the company faced. Indeed, the professional managers might have recognized that while they had worked hard to keep the problems from the founders, in doing so, they had failed to help the founders understand the severity of the problems and therefore the critical need to address them. Moreover, as they tried to explain the problems to the founders and therefore why IZIO provided so much opportunity, the professional managers would likely have realized that the founders were not as they had come to accuse them of being—power hungry, immature kids who didn't understand the realities of business and were determined to pursue notes at all costs. Rather, the founders would likely have been receptive to the professional managers' concerns and indeed acted as the talented, reasonable, level-headed people the professional managers had been so excited to join only a few months earlier.

Had any one dared to effectively express his differences in the vision meeting, he most likely could have started to repair the lost trust and respect, and taken the first step toward turning the vicious silent spiral into a more virtuous spiral of speaking up. An open, honest exchange of perspectives would likely have helped them all to appreciate how little they each currently understood where the others were coming from and how much they stood to learn from one another. However, to further achieve a deeper understanding of one another's perspectives would have required that beyond the vision meeting they continue to take the time necessary to effectively explore their differences—even in the face of immense time pressure. Indeed, if they came to recognize that silencing their differences would neither preserve their relationships nor enable them to get their tasks done as expeditiously as possible, and instead, they started to speak openly about their differences, it might have enabled them to position their company as something profitable. They might never have sold the company to CollegeClub and certainly would have responded differently to the sudden requirement that they move to San Diego. If only they had realized the destructive costs of silence and learned to express their differences, the story of Versity.com might have had a different ending. Without them having tried to seek mutual understanding, however, we'll never know what might have been.

ENDNOTES

INTRODUCTION

1. I should be clear that at the time I did not know that these people were harming their relationships. I observed them silencing their differences, but only after following the company's whole life cycle and returning home to analyze my field notes did I come to appreciate the profound costs of how they had acted. What I learned from this study is how destructive silencing can be and how hard it can be to detect the effects of silenced conflict for quite some time.

2. As Jean Bartunek and her colleagues note, covering over differences rather than confronting them openly is a common tendency: "In the public space of organizations . . . conflict is kept in check and masked through shared conventions that keep it from open view. Meetings are marked by civil discourse; personal attacks are whispered behind closed doors" (J. Bartunek, D. Kolb, and R. Lewicki, "Bringing conflict out from behind the scenes: Private, informal, and nonrational dimensions of conflict in organizations," in D. Kolb and J. Bartunek, eds., *Hidden Conflict in Organizations*, Newbury Park, Calif.: Sage, 1992, p. 213).

3. Silencing conflict integrates two core concepts—silencing and conflict. Research on conflict has a long history in the social sciences. Indeed, the focus of "conflict sociology" is on the fundamental cleavages dividing society—e.g., social class, status groups,

race, and gender. (See R. Collins, *Conflict Sociology: Toward an Explanatory Science,* New York: Academic Press, 1975.)

Recently, research on silencing has also received much attention. A review by Elizabeth Morrison and Frances Milliken provides an extensive analysis of the existing literature on silencing in organizations and further develops a theory of organizational silence (E. W. Morrison and F. J. Milliken, "Organizational silence: A barrier to change and development in a pluralistic world," *Academy of Management Review,* vol. 25, no. 4, 2000, pp. 706–725).

4. Mary Parker Follett, one of the founders of the field of conflict management and negotiation, wrote, "Think of [conflict] not as warfare but the appearance of difference, difference of opinion, of interests. For that is what conflict means—difference" (M. P. Follett, "Creative collaboration," in Pauline Graham, ed., *Prophet in Management,* Boston: Harvard Business School Press, 1995, p. 67; paper originally presented to the Bureau of Personnel Administration conference group in January 1925).

Research and theory on interpersonal and intragroup conflict distinguish between two types of conflict: task and relationship (see H. Guetzkow and J. Gyr, "An analysis of conflict in decision making groups," *Human Relations,* vol. 7, 1954, pp. 367–338; R. Priem and K. Price, "Process and outcome expectations for the dialectical inquiry, devil's advocacy, and consensus techniques of strategic decision making," *Group and Organization Studies,* vol. 16, 1991, pp. 206–225).

In *When You Say Yes But Mean No,* I am focusing only on conflicts—or differences—that start as *task* conflicts, which are conflicts that pertain to a difference of opinion or ideas about the task itself. Task conflicts may and often do evolve into relationship conflicts—conflicts that are purely emotional and that involve personal issues such as dislike of another person and feelings such as annoyance, frustration, and irritation. I describe that process further in Chapter 3. (For more details about different types of conflict, see K. Jehn and E. Mannix, "The dynamic nature of conflict: A longitudinal study of intragroup conflict and group performance," *Academy of Management Journal,* vol. 44, no. 2, 2001, pp. 238–251.)

5. Silencing conflict falls under the rubric of what Chris

Argyris refers to as a "defensive routine," whereby we create undiscussables and also make their undiscussability undiscussable. Defensive routines form a sort of protective shell around our deepest assumptions, defending us against pain but also keeping us from learning about the causes of that pain. (C. Argyris, *Overcoming Organizational Defenses*, Upper Saddle River, N.J.: Prentice Hall, 1990.)

6. The most pernicious result of difference is *escalation of conflict*. This is an intense and destructive engagement of difference. As conflict escalates, several changes may occur: the conflict becomes "heavier" (i.e., attempts to influence become more forceful, such as the use of threats), more energy and time are invested in the conflict, the issues become more general, more people become involved, and/or the parties' initial interests become overshadowed by a desire to hurt one another. Escalation of conflict can start small and in the end result in the destruction of relationships and organizations. War is the most extreme form of conflict escalation in which value—in the form of human lives—is destroyed. (See D. Pruitt and J. Rubin, *Social Conflict: Escalation, Stalemate, and Settlement*, New York: Random House, 1986.)

7. Conflict has been described as essential for effectively functioning societies, groups, and interpersonal relationships. The great pioneers of sociology—Karl Marx, Max Weber, George Simmel—argued that difference is not only unavoidable in society, it is essential for cultures to thrive. More recent sociologists who focus on the role of conflict have noted the importance of conflict at the group level. Lewis Coser wrote: "No group can be entirely harmonious. Groups require disharmony as well as harmony, dissociation as well as association; and conflicts within them are by no means altogether disruptive factors. . . . Far from being necessarily dysfunctional, a certain degree of conflict is an essential element" (L. A. Coser, *The Functions of Social Conflict*, Glencoe, Ill.: Free Press, 1956, p. 31).

Not only is conflict essential to robust societies and groups, social scientists studying meaningful and productive interpersonal relationships have found it to be a core component. Richard Walton, for example, explains that the benefits of conflict include an increase in motivation and energy to accomplish tasks, greater innovativeness, a better understanding of one's own position, and heightened awareness of one's own identity (R. E. Walton, *Interpersonal Peacemaking: Confrontations and Third Party Consultation,* Reading, Mass.: Addison-Wesley, 1969, p. 5).

8. The purpose of collaboration is to bring opposing sides together to realize their respective goals in a win-win outcome, or to take their differing perspectives and use them in a synergistic way to achieve an end result that is better than any of the initial perspectives. For discussions on collaboration, see, for example, B. Gray, *Collaborating: Finding Common Ground for Multiparty Problems,* San Francisco: Jossey-Bass, 1989; D. S. Hanson, *Cultivating Common Ground,* Boston: Butterworth-Heinemann, 1997; R. Hargrove, *Mastering the Art of Creative Collaboration,* New York: McGraw-Hill, 1998; L. A. Hill, "Leadership as collective genius," in S. Chowdhury, ed., *Management 21C,* New York: Prentice Hall, 2000; V. John-Steiner, *Creative Collaboration,* New York: Oxford University Press, 2000.

9. Kathleen Ryan and Daniel Oestreich discuss the high costs associated with an organizational environment of fear and silence. Employees in such an environment may experience physical ailments as well as loss of motivation, lack of extra effort, and contemplated or real job transfers; they may even resort to sabotage. (K. D. Ryan and D. K. Oestreich, *Driving Fear Out of the Workplace,* San Francisco: Jossey-Bass, 1998.)

For a review of the consequences of organizational silence on decision making, change processes, and employee well-being, see also Morrison and Milliken, "Organizational silence" (note 3 above).

10. Jean Baker Miller and Irene Stiver point out that people often adopt strategies for interacting that involve not being their true self in relationships. People use such strategies because they believe that these strategies will help preserve a sense of connection in the relationship. One such strategy is acting in a certain way just to please the other person—for example, if we think the other person wants to relate only to someone who is always happy, we act happy when around that person, even when we are sad or upset. Although Miller and Stiver don't specifically mention silencing difference as a strategy, it certainly fits under their notion of an inter-

action strategy that involves holding back one's true self to preserve connection in the relationship. Miller and Stiver further suggest that these strategies meant to preserve connection generally create the opposite of what is desired: they create disconnection in the relationship. Miller and Stiver call this the "central relational paradox." What happens is that when one does not act authentically—that is, according to one's true self—there is little chance for connection, as connection requires authenticity. Without authenticity, one can only experience disconnection. (J. B. Miller and I. P. Stiver, *The Healing Connection*, Boston: Beacon Press, 1997.)

Jerry Harvey proposes a similar paradox in his discussion of the "Abilene Paradox." He suggests that sometimes organization members agree in private about the nature of the situation and what steps are required to cope with it. Yet the members fail to accurately communicate their desires or beliefs to each other; indeed, they do the opposite, leading one another to misperceive the collective reality. As a result, they take actions contrary to what they want to do and arrive at results that are often counterproductive to the organization's intents and purposes. Moreover, as a result of taking counterproductive actions, they further experience frustration, anger, and irritation, and end up blaming authority figures and one another. (J. Harvey, "The Abilene Paradox: The management of agreement," *Organizational Dynamics,* Summer 1974, pp. 63–80.)

11. In the late nineteenth century, Mary Parker Follett recognized the destructive consequences of silencing conflict, noting, "The ignoring of differences is the most fatal mistake in politics or industry or international life: Every difference that is swept up into a bigger conception feeds and enriches society; every difference which is ignored feeds *on* society and eventually corrupts it" (M. P. Follett, *The New State,* University Park: Pennsylvania State University Press, 1998, p. 40).

12. Albert Hirschman describes three possible responses individuals can have to dissatisfaction in an organization—exit, voice, and loyalty. *Exit* is permanent movement away from the organization (e.g., quitting a job), whereas *voice* involves attempts to improve the situation. *Loyalty* involves a belief that things will improve and ranges from passively assuming that someone else will

take action to improve things to actively supporting the organiza-
tion. (A. O. Hirschman, *Exit, Voice and Loyalty: Responses to
Decline in Firms, Organizations, and States,* Cambridge: Harvard
University Press, 1970.)

Caryl Rusbult, Isabella Zambrodt, and Lawanna Gunn have
added a fourth response to dissatisfaction: *neglect,* which an individual shows by putting in less effort, not working at a relationship, and letting it fall apart. Whereas loyalty involves the belief
that things will improve, neglect does not. (C. E. Rusbult, I. M.
Zambrodt, and L. K. Gunn, "Exit, voice, loyalty and neglect:
Responses to dissatisfaction in romantic involvements," *Journal of
Personality and Social Psychology,* vol. 43, 1982, pp. 1230–1242.)

The notion of silence described in *When You Say Yes But
Mean No* is closest to a passive kind of loyalty (not voicing oneself
but believing things will get better) and sometimes results in
neglect or exit when one loses hope that the relationship can be
saved. However, whereas Hirschman focuses on exit, voice, and
loyalty, I focus on what happens when we are loyal and don't voice
our differences and thus end up either neglecting (what I call
"withdrawing from") or exiting from the relationship.

13. Throughout my research at Versity, people often confided
in me about their thoughts and feelings. I tried to play a neutral
role, acting as a sounding board, neither agreeing with their complaints (a destructive role—facilitating gossip—that I describe in
Chapter 11) nor helping them to think through their situations and
what to say and do (a constructive role that I suggest that we might
want to ask third parties to play).

CHAPTER ONE

1. Many scholars have noted the common tendency for
reviewers to silence their opinions when giving performance feedback—and how that silencing undermines the purpose of the performance review process. Louis Barnes, for example, argues that
when people give performance feedback, all too often they do not
say what they really think because they do not want to hurt the
other person. Barnes goes on to give some suggestions for how to
make the performance feedback process more valuable for those

involved—such as establishing ground rules for the feedback discussion, emphasizing specific and recent examples of performance, and focusing on issues that the other person can actually do something about. (L. B. Barnes, "Managing interpersonal feedback," Harvard Business School Teaching Note, 1982.)

For additional thoughts on giving performance feedback, see also M. Beer, "Conducting a performance appraisal interview," Harvard Business School Teaching Note, 1997; M. A. Peiperl, "Getting 360-degree feedback right," *Harvard Business Review,* vol. 79, January 2001, pp. 142–147.

2. Although Robert Blake and Jane Mouton focus on managerial styles, not particular actions as I do, a manager's act of trying to silence an employee is characteristic of what they call the 9,1 management style. The 9,1 management style has a high concern for production and a low concern for people. When dealing with subordinates, managers with this orientation focus on direction and control. Authority and hierarchy are not to be questioned. If a subordinate were to question a 9,1-oriented manager, the manager might reply with something like, "These are your instructions. Do them and don't give me any lip" (R. R. Blake and J. S. Mouton, *The Managerial Grid: Key Orientations for Achieving Production Through People,* Houston: Gulf Publishing, 1964, p. 20).

Such an answer is similar to what I label "suppressing." In fact, Blake and Mouton specifically say that suppression is the "fundamental rule of the game" when it comes to managing conflict in the 9,1 managerial style because conflict is not tolerated and simply has to be cut off (ibid., p. 30).

3. Chris Argyris refers to glossing over a conflict, rather than openly dealing with it, as a "bypass." A bypass is a strategy employed to avoid discussing an issue that might be threatening or embarrassing to one or more of the parties. Bypasses are designed to work past rather than through a problem, and a successful bypass not only will subvert discussion of the problem but will itself be covered over and not discussed. (C. Argyris, *Overcoming Organizational Defenses,* Upper Saddle River, N.J.: Prentice Hall, 1990.)

Characteristics of Blake and Mouton's 1,9 managerial style also pertain to what I label acts of glossing. Blake and Mouton describe the 1,9 management style as having a low concern for production and a high concern for people. This style values harmony and togetherness, and the work unit is seen as "one big happy family" (Blake and Mouton, *Managerial Grid,* p. 62; note 2 above). A manager operating according to a 1,9 style avoids disagreement, negative emotions, rejection, and frustration by smoothing over or glossing over the issue. Blake and Mouton use both the terms *smoothing over* and *glossing over* to refer to the various ways a manager operating with a 1,9 style deals with conflict. I note this because I, in contrast, use the term *smoothing over* as a subtype of *glossing over.*

1. When people are new to a group or organization, they must learn the norms or expectations of being a member—what we often refer to as "learning the ropes" (see J. Van Maanen and E. Schein, "Toward a theory of organizational socialization," in B. M. Staw, ed., *Research in Organizational Behavior,* vol. 1, Greenwich, Conn.: JAI Press, 1979, pp. 209–264).

2. The discussion of norms in this chapter is deliberately vague with respect to the topics of conversation that the norms are applied to. Norms can be quite complicated in the sense that a norm of silence does not necessarily apply equally to all topics or all people in a given situation. There are multiple variations. Karen Jehn has found that in some groups, for instance, there may be a norm to not talk about relationship conflicts, yet expressing differences over tasks is acceptable (K. A. Jehn, "A qualitative analysis of conflict types and dimensions in organizational groups," *Administrative Science Quarterly,* vol. 42, 1997, pp. 530–557).

Moreover, scholars who study intergroup relations and diversity in organizations argue that different cultural identity groups have different norms and that organization or group norms may apply differently to people from different identity groups (see, e.g., C. P. Alderfer and K. K. Smith, "Studying intergroup relations embedded in organizations," *Administrative Science Quarterly,* vol. 27, 1982, pp. 35–65; T. H. Cox, *Cultural Diversity in Organi-*

zations: Theory, Research, and Practice, San Francisco: Berrett-Koehler, 1993).

3. Past research suggests that groups develop norms about whether or not conflict is tolerated. Members of groups with norms of not tolerating conflicting viewpoints tend to quickly stifle creative exchanges of ideas, whereas those in groups with norms of openness encourage one another to express their doubts, opinions, and uncertainties. (See, e.g., J. M. Brett, "Negotiating group decisions," *Negotiation Journal,* vol. 7, 1991, pp. 291–310.)

4. In addition to the kinds of norms described in this chapter—organization, group, and interpersonal norms—there are many other kinds of norms that may also affect silencing. For instance, the norms of national cultures (i.e., norms that are prevalent across an entire national culture, such as individualism or collectivism) or the norms of particular occupations (i.e., norms that govern occupational groups, such as engineers or salespeople) may include norms that lead people to silence.

5. The effect of organizational culture on individuals' tendency to silence has been addressed by multiple authors (see, e.g., C. Argyris, "Double loop learning in organizations," *Harvard Business Review,* vol. 55, no. 5, 1977, pp. 115–129; E. W. Morrison and F. J. Milliken, "Organizational silence: A barrier to change and development in a pluralistic world," *Academy of Management Review,* vol. 25, no. 4, 2000, pp. 706–725; K. D. Ryan and D. K. Oestreich, *Driving Fear Out of the Workplace,* San Francisco: Jossey-Bass, 1998).

6. In *The Executive Way,* Calvin Morrill reports on nearly two years of ethnographic research among executives in thirteen corporations (C. Morrill, *The Executive Way: Conflict Management in Corporations,* Chicago: University of Chicago Press, 1995). Morrill found that norms about how people deal with conflict were heavily influenced by the underlying organizational form. He found that conflict management in mechanistic bureaucracies (i.e., "Institutionalized structures of authority . . . within which managers adhere to the prerogatives of superiors as defined by formal chains of command, distinct spheres of influence and expertise, and behavioral predictability," ibid., p. 46) is constituted in its

authority structure and varies according to the rank of its partici-pants within the chain of command. As one executive vice presi-dent in a mechanistic bureaucracy explained, "No matter how high you get in the organization, you have to live the chain of command, not get out of control, control your reports [subordinates], all the while trying to get to the next slot" (ibid., p. 92). In contrast, in atomistic organizations (i.e., organizations "in which lone practi-tioners ply their disciplines with tightly controlled staffs," ibid., p. 52), Morrill found that official rank had little influence on conflict management. Top managers in atomistic organizations primarily avoid one another as means of expressing and pursuing their issues. As one senior partner in an atomistic organization described, "Young associates hover around their managers and partners working as hard as they can, doing this and doing that, running off-site, flying a red-eye here and there. Partners aren't much different. A lot of the work is done behind closed doors; it's really quiet here" (ibid., p. 141).

7. David Thomas and Robin Ely identified paradigms (or col-lections of norms) that dominate the thinking and valuing of diversity in organizations. The "discrimination-and-fairness" par-adigm views diversity as a moral imperative. People with this per-spective seek to build a diverse workforce but don't see diversity as important for the work of the group or organization. In contrast, the "integration-and-learning" paradigm links diversity to work processes—it considers the voicing of difference as essential for performing the core work of the group or organization. Thomas and Ely have further found that which paradigm is dominant in an organization determines whether diversity itself leads to positive outcomes (e.g., collaboration and learning) or negative ones (e.g., tensions). When the "discrimination-and-fairness" paradigm is dominant, diversity results in negative outcomes; when the "inte-gration-and-learning" paradigm is dominant, diversity results in positive outcomes. (R. J. Ely and D. A. Thomas, "Cultural diversity at work: The effects of diversity perspectives on work group processes and outcomes," *Administrative Science Quarterly,* vol. 46, 2001, pp. 229–273; D. A. Thomas and R. J. Ely, "Making dif-ferences matter: A new paradigm for managing diversity," *Harvard Business Review,* vol. 74, September–October 1996, pp. 79–90.)

8. Patricia Hewlin showed this *Dilbert* cartoon as part of her opening remarks at an Academy of Management symposium in Denver, Colorado, in August 2002. The cartoon comes from Scott Adams, *The Dilbert Principle,* New York: HarperBusiness, 1996, p. 85.

9. Charles Redding describes how many companies want employees to be "loyal," meaning that the companies want people who will "internalize the corporate goals and values." Loyal employees are those who do not rock the boat by expressing dissent. (W. C. Redding, "Rocking boats, blowing whistles, and teaching speech communication," *Communication Education,* vol. 34, 1985, pp. 245–258; quote from p. 245.)

Jo Sprague and Gary Ruud argue similarly that although some organizations are relatively receptive to dissenting opinions, many are not and view dissent as a serious violation of loyalty. Sprague and Ruud found that employees are very aware of how a dissenting opinion is likely to be perceived by management. When employees perceive that a dissenting opinion is likely to be seen negatively, they typically choose not to speak up because they fear some kind of retaliation. (J. Sprague and G. Ruud, "Boat-rocking in the high-technology culture," *American Behavioral Scientist,* vol. 32, no. 2, 1988, pp. 169–193.)

10. Irving Janis, in his analysis of the phenomenon of "groupthink"—which is specifically focused on group decision making—describes how pressure to conform to the group can prevent members from expressing dissenting opinions. Groupthink occurs whenever group members strive for cohesiveness and unanimity to the extent that it overrides their motivation to realistically examine different courses of action. When groupthink is operating, members don't express doubts or unpopular views out of a desire to maintain cohesiveness. According to Janis, close-knit groups are particularly prone to the group pressures associated with groupthink. (I. Janis, *Groupthink,* Boston: Houghton Mifflin, 1982.)

11. John Gabarro argues that one of the dimensions along which relationships develop is "uniqueness of interaction"—that is, interactions by two people in a relationship are idiosyncratic to those two people. According to Gabarro, these interactions are guided by norms or mutual expectations that develop over time

through a set of stages: orientation, exploration, testing, and stabilization. In the first stage, "orientation," relationship partners form impressions of each other. The second stage, "exploration," is a more intense stage of exploration and learning about each other. In the "testing" stage, the relationship partners test the limits of trust and influence, so that by the "stabilization" stage, they have arrived at a mutual set of expectations and interpersonal norms. (J. J. Gabarro, "The development of working relationships," In J. W. Lorsch, ed., *Handbook of Organizational Behavior,* Englewood Cliffs, NJ: Prentice-Hall, 1987, pp. 172–189.)

12. Erving Goffman argues that the beginning of a relationship establishes how each person will act toward the other, a pattern that over time becomes increasingly difficult to change without jeopardizing the relationship. As Goffman puts it, "The initial definition of the situation projected by an individual tends to provide a plan for the co-operative activity that follows" (E. Goffman, *The Presentation of Self in Everyday Life,* New York: Anchor Books, 1959, p. 12).

13. Harry Stack Sullivan argues that this socialization happens through the use of anxiety, which he defines as an "anticipated unfavorable appraisal of one's current activity by someone whose opinion is significant." According to Sullivan, this practice is utilized in all cultures to train humans to become functioning members—according to the values and beliefs of the particular culture. (H. S. Sullivan, *The Interpersonal Theory of Psychiatry,* New York: Norton, 1953; quote from p. 113.)

14. The most common reasons scholars cite for why people don't speak up have to do with fears—e.g., fears of negative labels, losing their job or reputation, or rejection (see, e.g., J. Harvey, "The Abilene Paradox: The management of agreement," *Organizational Dynamics,* Summer 1974, pp. 63–80; F. J. Milliken, E. W. Morrison, and P. F. Hewlin, "Choosing to stay silent at work: What employees don't speak about and why," working paper, New York University, Stern School of Business, 2002; Ryan and Oestreich, *Driving Fear Out of the Workplace* [note 5 above]).

15. William Felstiner, Richard Abel, and Austin Sarat talk about the individual personality variables that can affect whether one makes a legal grievance or claim, which is a formalized form of

speaking up. The variables they identify include risk preferences, contentiousness, and feelings about personal efficacy, privacy, independence, and attachment. They also identify social structural variables (e.g., class, ethnicity, gender, and age) and variables having to do with the relationship between the parties (e.g., sphere of social life that brings them together, their relative status, and history of prior conflict) that shape the way in which the parties conduct themselves. (W. L. F. Felstiner, R. L. Abel, and A. Sarat, "The emergence and transformation of disputes: naming, blaming and claiming," *Law and Society Review*, vol. 15, 1980–1981, pp. 631–654.)

16. The concept of "face" comes from Erving Goffman. Goffman takes a dramaturgical approach to exploring how people behave in social situations. That is, he uses the metaphor of the world as a theater and considers individuals as "actors" who interact through "performances" that are shaped by the environment and the audience. When actors perform, they behave in ways that portray who they claim to be in terms of positive social attributes. One's "face" is the image of self that one claims by acting in particular ways. (Goffman, *The Presentation of Self* [note 12 above]; ibid., *Interaction Ritual: Essays on Face-to-Face-Behavior*, New York: Pantheon Books, 1967.)

Renee Tynan and her colleagues further explore what they call "face threat sensitivity," which they define as "the likelihood that an individual will have a negative affective reaction to a threat to his or her social image" (J. White, R. Tynan, A. Galinsky, and L. Thompson, "Face threat sensitivity in negotiations: Roadblock to agreement and joint gain," working paper, Dartmouth College, 2002, p. 4). Tynan's research suggests that people who have a high degree of face threat sensitivity are less likely to communicate openly and directly with others and that others are also less likely to be honest with them and tend to perceive them as less trustworthy (R. Tynan, "The impact of threat sensitivity and face giving on upward communication in organizational hierarchies," paper presented at Academy of Management Conference, Chicago, 1999).

17. Research on shyness, for example, suggests that shy people have a strong fear of disapproval. So, to avoid disapproval, shy people adopt self-protective strategies when interacting with others.

They tend not to disclose much information about themselves and come across as quiet, inhibited, and withdrawn in social interactions. When they do speak, they tend to conform more to what they think is expected of them and will moderate their judgments when they think they might be confronted by someone with a strong and/or different viewpoint. (See, e.g., R. M. Arkin, E. A. Lake, and A. H. Baumgardner, "Shyness and self presentation," in W. Jones, J. Cheek, and S. Briggs, eds., *Shyness: Perspectives on Research and Treatment,* New York: Plenum Press, 1986, pp. 189–203; K. G. A. Meleshko and L. E. Alden, "Anxiety and self disclosure: Toward a motivational model," *Journal of Personality and Social Psychology,* vol. 64, 1993, pp. 1000–1009.)

18. Power based on resource dependency is a sociological view of power. According to this view, power is a property of the relationship rather than an attribute of an individual. Power resides implicitly in the other person's dependency—that is, we have power to the extent that the other person is dependent on us for something valuable that they desire, such as love, approval, or career rewards. For a discussion of this perspective on power, see R. M. Emerson, "Power-dependence relations," *American Sociological Review,* vol. 17, 1962, pp. 31–41.

19. I suggest that how people are situated within the social networks of an organization—e.g., how well connected they are, what structural position they are in—may make a difference in whether they speak up. This suggestion is drawn from work by Jane Dutton and her colleagues following their extensive research on the reasons why people decide whether to speak up about particular issues to upper-level managers in their organization. Although Dutton and her colleagues have not yet empirically examined the question of how one's structural position affects issue selling, their suggestion builds on earlier research by David Krackhardt that suggests that people in different positions in the organization have different vantage points on informal social networks and that those different perspectives impact people's use of informal networks. (J. Dutton, S. Ashford, K. Lawrence, and K. Miner-Rubino, "Red light, green light: Making sense of the organizational context for issue selling," *Organization Science,* vol. 13, 2002, pp. 355–369; D. Krackhardt, "Assessing the political

landscape: structure, cognition, and power in organizations," *Administrative Science Quarterly,* vol. 31, pp. 342–369.)

20. For a discussion of identity groups, see C. P. Alderfer, "An intergroup perspective on group dynamics," in J. W. Lorsch, ed., *Handbook of Organizational Behavior,* Englewood Cliffs, N.J.: Prentice Hall, 1987. Alderfer notes that individuals are not all affected by group membership in the same way. Although every individual belongs to a set of identity groups, which groups are important and salient to any one person varies. And some groups may be important to a person at one particular time whereas others are important to that same person at another time. A person's perceptions and interactions will be influenced most by whatever group is most important and salient to that individual at a given moment.

Alderfer also describes the critical role of power for understanding intergroup relations. He states that "the analysis of intergroup relations is in part a study of power relations among groups" (C. P. Alderfer, "Group and intergroup relations," in J. R. Hackman and J. L. Suttle, eds., *Improving Life at Work: Behavioral Science Approaches to Organizational Science,* Santa Monica, Calif.: Goodyear Publishing, 1977, p. 241).

The relative power and status differences among identity groups within an organization don't arise in a vacuum. Rather, they are produced by the status value that the larger society ascribes to those identity groups. (See, e.g., C. L. Ridgeway, "The social construction of status value: Gender and other nominal characteristics," *Social Forces,* vol. 70, 1991, pp. 367–386.)

21. This example is drawn from Ely and Thomas, "Cultural diversity at work" (note 7 above).

22. In their study on employee silencing, Frances Milliken, Elizabeth Morrison, and Pat Hewlin describe this kind of mental calculus. They found that people ask themselves, "What is likely to happen if I speak up?" when deciding whether to speak up. To answer this question, people draw from past experiences, stored knowledge, and what they have seen and heard from others. When employees perceive that speaking up is likely to yield positive outcomes, then they will be motivated to choose that option. If, however, the likelihood of negative outcomes is perceived to be high

(and/or the likelihood of positive outcomes low), there will be little motivation to speak up. (Milliken, Morrison, and Hewlin, "Choosing to stay silent at work"; note 14 above.)

23. Research on organizations and groups has found that a person is more likely to speak up or make a change when they perceive that the other is open and accepting. For instance, in their research on middle managers' efforts to sell issues to top managers, Jane Dutton and her colleagues found that middle managers were more likely to attempt to sell an issue when they perceived that top management was willing to listen (J. Dutton, S. Ashford, R. O'Neill, E. Hayes, and E. Wierba, "Reading the wind: How middle managers assess the context for selling issues to top management," *Strategic Management Journal,* vol. 18, 1997, pp. 407–423).

Similarly, Elizabeth Morrison found that an employee's perception of how open top management is to new ideas and change impacts the employee's decision on whether to attempt to initiate some kind of change (E. W. Morrison, "Taking charge at work: Extrarole efforts to initiate workplace change," *Academy of Management Journal,* vol. 42, 1999, pp. 403–419).

24. Jerry Harvey argues that one reason why people silence conflict is that they focus on the *possibility* that negative consequences could result rather than the *probability* that they will (Harvey, "The Abilene Paradox"; note 14 above).

25. Edgar Schein points out that there is room for variation even within the constraints of a norm (E. Schein, *Process Consultation Revisited: Building the Helping Relationship,* Reading, Mass.: Addison-Wesley, 1999).

John Van Maanen further points out the possibility of violating a norm and moreover the potential for creating change in the process. He provides a detailed account of the costs and benefits of such deviance. (J. Van Maanen, "The self, situation, and the rules of interpersonal relations," in W. Bennis, J. Van Maanen, E. Schein, and R. Steele, eds., *Essays in Interpersonal Dynamics,* Homewood, Ill.: Dorsey Press, 1979, pp. 43–101.)

26. Norms are not clear, external realities—rather, they are constructed through people's day-to-day interactions. The idea that the way we behave when interacting with others creates and

reinforces norms is reminiscent of Harold Garfinkel's research. Garfinkel looked closely at conversations and showed how norms are the product of the ongoing interaction among the people involved. He further showed that often our awareness of a norm arises only when someone behaves differently from our expectations. When this happens, one way to understand the situation is to reason that the other person is outside the norm. Garfinkel argues that we—in collaboration with others—create the social reality of the norm and carry it with us in the form of expectations in future interactions. Garfinkel further argues that norms therefore are not clear external realities—rather they are constructed through people's day-to-day interactions. (H. Garfinkel, *Studies in Ethnomethodology*, Cambridge: Polity Press, 1967.)

27. Karl Weick outlines the properties of sensemaking. Sensemaking begins with the sensemaker, the person doing the sensemaking. We make sense of what is going on around us in light of who we are, while at the same time who we are depends on the context. To engage in sensemaking is to construct, filter, and create the world in which we live. The fact that sensemaking is social is also important. We don't make sense in isolation but in relation to others. We act either in the presence of others or with the awareness that our actions will be implemented, understood, or approved by others. Sensemaking is also ongoing. We are always in the middle of the process—always gathering information that affects how we act—and how we act is affecting the reality of the situation about which we are gathering information. But we cannot gather this information and process it without some filtering. We focus on the cues that are most salient to us—these cues are not the answer, but they point in certain directions. There is also a strong reflexive quality to this process. People make sense of things by seeing a world in which they have already imposed what they believe. As Weick notes, "How can I know what I think until I see what I say?" The final property of sensemaking is that it is driven by plausibility rather than by accuracy. We need to know only enough to get on with our projects. (K. Weick, *Sensemaking in Organizations*, Thousand Oaks, Calif.: Sage, 1995, pp. 17–62; quote from p. 18.)

28. When people don't speak up because of a norm of silence, they are conforming to that norm. According to Charles Kiesler

and Sara Kiesler, conformity can be defined as a shift in one's position—whether beliefs, values, and/or behavior—to a different position as a result of real or imagined social pressure (C. A. Kiesler and S. B. Kiesler, *Conformity*, Reading, Mass.: Addison-Wesley, 1969).

29. There are people such as Elizabeth Morrison and Frances Milliken at the Stern School of Business at New York University who are further investigating this question. Morrison and Milliken argue that when certain characteristics are present in top management (e.g., long average tenure) and in the organization and its environment (e.g., the organization is in a stable industry and adopts a low-cost strategy), managers develop a fear of negative feedback and believe that employees are self-interested, that management knows best, and that unity is good. These fears and beliefs among management lead to structures (e.g., centralized decision making), policies (e.g., lack of formal upward feedback mechanisms), and practices (e.g., tendency to reject dissent) that give employees the message that their voice is not welcome—thereby creating a climate of silence in which employees believe that speaking up is not worth the effort and/or that expressing opinions can be dangerous. (Morrison and Milliken, "Organizational silence"; note 5 above.)

CHAPTER THREE

1. Arlie Hochschild focuses on the emotional work that people do to maintain an image—for instance, one of agreement. Emotional work involves: a *cognitive* effort to change the image, idea, or thought; a *bodily* effort to change the somatic, or physical, symptoms of emotion; and an *expressive* effort to change the gestures (e.g., smiling and nodding). (A. Hochschild, "Emotion work, feeling rules and social structure," *American Journal of Sociology,* 1979, vol. 85, no. 3, pp. 551–575; A. Hochschild, *The Managed Heart,* Berkeley and Los Angeles: University of California Press, 1983.)

2. Cognitive dissonance theory, originated by Leon Festinger, asserts that individuals feel tension when they experience inconsistent cognitions. These cognitions can be beliefs, preferences, opin-

ions, or even knowledge of one's feelings or behavior. When an individual holds a belief but behaves in a way that is inconsistent with that belief, that inconsistency will cause the individual to feel tension. (L. Festinger, *A Theory of Cognitive Dissonance,* Palo Alto, Calif.: Stanford University Press, 1957.)

This tension from cognitive dissonance is different from the tension that stems from having an unresolved conflict with another person—but it may be an additional source of tension in silencing conflict. That is, when individuals silence conflict, they experience tension from the unresolved conflict, and they also experience tension from the cognitive dissonance between what they say (and don't say) and what they think and feel.

3. Many scholars have described the idea that not revealing one's true self leads to anxiety and negative feelings. Some who study authenticity have noted that there may be psychological tension between the display of a "false self" and one's "true self." People feel that they are displaying a "false self" when they don't verbally express their thoughts, opinions, and feelings. (See, e.g., S. Harter, "Authenticity," in C. R. Snyder and S. J. Lopez, eds., *Handbook of Positive Psychology,* Oxford: Oxford University Press, 2002, pp. 382–394.)

Psychologists who conduct research on self-disclosure have further found that not disclosing information about ourselves to others—descriptive information as well as thoughts, feelings, and beliefs—increases physiological stress and anxiety. One possible reason for this is that holding information in forces us to obsess about it—simply because we are focusing our energies on keeping the information in. (See, e.g., V. J. Derlega, S. Metts, S. Petronio, and S. T. Margulis, *Self Disclosure,* Newbury Park, Calif.: Sage, 1993.)

4. In *The Dance of Anger,* Harriet Lerner describes the well of anger that builds when one does not express oneself. She argues that by putting another person's wishes or opinions ahead of our own, we are "de-selfing." This de-selfing—or hiding our voice—in and of itself causes us to feel angry. (H. Lerner, *The Dance of Anger,* New York: Harper & Row, 1985.)

Similarly, in *Silencing the Self,* Dana Crowley Jack points out that many women experience loss of self and anger as a result of silencing themselves. Because women tend to believe they are always supposed to be pleasant and nice, they silence any thoughts and feelings they have that don't fit into that perceived expectation. As a result, they lose their sense of self and feel angry and resentful. Moreover, they believe that they can't share those negative feelings, thus compounding their silencing and the resulting negative emotions. (D. C. Jack, *Silencing the Self,* New York: HarperPerennial, 1991.)

5. Freud conceived of human beings as holding a vast reservoir of psychic energy—internal forces of tension, frustration, aggression, and sexuality—that if not released will be displaced through less direct channels (as described by J. Kottler in *Beyond Blame: A New Way of Resolving Conflicts in Relationships,* San Francisco: Jossey-Bass, 1994, pp. 37–38).

6. It does very little good to blame someone else. In essence, we avoid any responsibility for and control over the situation. As a result, nothing gets settled. We each feel unheard or poorly treated. (D. Stone, B. Patton, and S. Heen, *Difficult Conversations,* New York: Penguin, 1999, p. 27; see also Kottler, *Beyond Blame,* p. 21 [note 5 above]; Lerner, *The Dance of Anger,* pp. 23–24 [note 4 above].)

7. Jeffrey Kottler explains that blame is a distortion of reality because it is highly unlikely that anything is ever entirely one person's fault (Kottler, *Beyond Blame,* p. 93; note 5 above).

8. Jeffrey Kottler describes how blaming oneself involves a tendency toward self-pity and helplessness and is just as counterproductive as blaming another person (Kottler, *Beyond Blame,* p. 83; note 5 above).

9. To protect this company's identity, "Printco" is a pseudonym.

10. Scholars have described both the sense of distance and the disconnection that can result within relationships. The idea of experiencing "distance" in a relationship comes from family systems theory. According to this theory, members of a social group shift between connection, or feeling "close," and separateness, or feeling "distant." Social distance is constructed in the minds of the relationship partners and may bear no relationship to physical distance—two people may feel close yet be halfway across the world

from each other, or they may feel distant and see each other every day. (See, e.g., C. B. Broderick, *Understanding Family Process,* Newbury Park, Calif.: Sage, 1993; D. Kantor and W. Lehr, *Inside the Family,* San Francisco: Jossey-Bass, 1975.) The experience of "disconnection" in a relationship is similar. Jean Baker Miller and Irene Stiver describe "disconnection" as what we experience when we feel cut off or emotionally separate from those with whom we share a relationship. Disconnection happens when we do not feel free to be authentic and to represent ourselves truthfully to the other person, so instead we act in a way that is different from how we truly feel and think—such as when we silence ourselves. According to Miller and Stiver, as long as we do not act according to how we truly feel and think, we will not be able to form a real connection with the other person, as real connection requires that we relate to others authentically. (J. B. Miller and I. P. Stiver, *The Healing Connection,* Boston: Beacon Press, 1997.)

11. Self-protectiveness involves both cognitive and emotional components—that is, both perceiving and feeling that one needs to protect oneself from any harm that the other person might inflict. Although research in cognitive psychology has traditionally investigated how people process information without much consideration of the role that emotions play in information processing, researchers now commonly accept that cognitions and emotions are deeply intertwined. (See, e.g., Z. Kunda, *Social Cognition: Making Sense of People,* Cambridge, Mass: MIT Press, 2002.)

12. Attribution theories in social cognition are based on the idea that people develop explanations for why events happen, such as why others behave as they do (see, e.g., I. Frieze, D. Bar-Tal, and J. Carroll, *New Approaches to Social Problems: Applications of Attribution Theory,* San Francisco: Jossey-Bass, 1979; S. Fiske and S. Taylor, *Social Cognition,* New York: McGraw-Hill, 1991; Kunda, *Social Cognition* [note 11 above]).

One well-documented bias in making attributions is the fundamental attribution error, which is the tendency to attribute another person's behavior to dispositional factors, such as their personality or other personal characteristics, rather than to the situation (F. Heider, *The Psychology of Interpersonal Relations,* New

York: Wiley, 1958; L. Ross, "The intuitive psychologist and his shortcomings: Distortions in the attribution process," in L. Berkowitz, ed., *Advances in Experimental Social Psychology,* New York: Academic Press, 1977, pp. 174–221).

13. Similar to the self-reinforcing pattern that I describe between self-protection and negative attribution, Catherine Durnell Cramton describes a cycle based on research of distributed work groups—that is, groups that work together from multiple locations via electronic communications. In such work groups, party A (a person or a sub-group) misinterprets what party B (another person or sub-group) says and does (e.g., not responding quickly to a question) and attributes the causes to something negative about party B (e.g., the person or sub-group is unwilling to work). These negative attributions cause party A to share less information with party B, which then leads to further misinterpretation and negative attributions. Thus, a self-perpetuating cycle develops. (C. D. Cramton, "The mutual knowledge problem and its consequences for dispersed collaboration," *Organization Science,* vol. 12, 2001, pp. 346–371.)

In *Driving Fear Out of the Workplace,* Kathleen Ryan and Daniel Oestreich further present a pattern of mistrust in which cycles of self-protection and negative attributions among managers and employees not only exist but intersect with one another. Ryan and Oestreich argue that managers and employees often make negative assumptions or attributions about each other (e.g., that the other is operating in their own self-interest). These negative attributions drive self-protective behaviors within each party. Yet, as each party acts in a self-protective manner, the other interprets that behavior as aggressive (that is, makes further negative attributions) and acts even more self-protectively as a result. (K. Ryan and D. Oestreich, *Driving Fear Out of the Workplace,* San Francisco: Jossey-Bass, 1998, p. 21.)

14. Both trust and psychological safety are elements of a relationship that affect risk taking within a relationship. In relationships characterized by trust, people are more willing to take risks and to make themselves vulnerable with one another; in relationships characterized by distrust, people are less willing to take risks and to make themselves vulnerable (see, e.g., G. Bigley and

J. Pearce, 1998, "Straining for shared meaning in organizational science: Problems of trust and distrust," *Academy of Management Review,* vol. 23, pp. 405–421).

Psychological safety is a related aspect of the relationship climate that affects interpersonal risk taking and breaking norms that silence. Focusing specifically on work teams, Amy Edmondson describes psychological safety as the "shared belief that the team is safe for interpersonal risk taking." She notes that in an interpersonal climate characterized by psychological safety, people believe that others will not reject or embarrass them when they speak up about difficult issues; in contrast, in a climate characterized by a lack of psychological safety, people will be more anxious about speaking up because of fear that the other will reject or embarrass them if they do. (A. Edmondson, "Psychological safety and learning behavior in work teams," *Administrative Science Quarterly,* vol. 44, 1999, pp. 350–383; quote from p. 354.)

CHAPTER FOUR

1. L. David Brown also refers to the dynamic of "withdrawal." He suggests that too little conflict in a relationship can take one of two forms—suppression or withdrawal. Suppression, according to Brown's definition, happens when two parties deny their differences and act as if their interests were all common, whereas withdrawal occurs when the parties avoid any problematic differences—for example, by minimizing interdependent activity. (L. D. Brown, *Managing Conflict at Organizational Interfaces,* Reading, Mass.: Addison-Wesley, 1983.)

Relating Brown's definitions to the dynamics of the silent spiral, suppression captures the relationship when it's still caught in the silent spiral. Withdrawal occurs after the breaking point, when the parties carry on with no perception of working together, but neither has completely exited the relationship.

2. W. A. Kahn describes disengagement at work as the "withdrawal and defense of a person's preferred self in behaviors that promote a lack of connections, physical, cognitive, and emotional absence, and passive, incomplete role performances" (W. A. Kahn, "Psychological conditions of personal engagement and disengage-

ment at work," *Academy of Management Journal,* vol. 33, no. 4, 1990, pp. 692–724; quote from p. 701).

3. Elizabeth Morrison and Frances Milliken argue that in an organizational climate of silence, people don't feel valued and perceive a lack of control. As a result, they lose motivation and satisfaction with their work and may withdraw from—or even leave—the organization. (E. W. Morrison and F. J. Milliken, "Organizational silence: A barrier to change and development in a pluralistic world," *Academy of Management Review,* vol. 25, no. 4, 2000, pp. 706–725.)

4. I should be clear that although it is valuable to recognize the potential benefits of expressing differences—such as creativity and learning—I am not advocating that more conflict is necessarily better than less. Rather, my primary focus is on what happens when conflict that already exists is not expressed—and one consequence of silencing conflict is that the potential for creativity and learning is adversely affected.

5. Teresa Amabile proposes that a product or a response is considered creative to the extent that (1) it is both novel and useful or valuable to the task at hand, and (2) the task itself is heuristic rather than algorithmic. A heuristic task is one in which there is no clear and readily identifiable path to the solution. Thus, creative activity involves discovering novel and useful solutions to heuristic tasks. (T. Amabile, *The Social Psychology of Creativity,* New York: Springer-Verlag, 1983.)

6. Dorothy Leonard and Walter Swap describe divergent thinking as "a breaking away from familiar, established ways of seeing and doing." It takes place when people consider an issue from various perspectives. (D. Leonard and W. Swap, *When Sparks Fly: Igniting Creativity in Groups,* Boston: Harvard Business School Press, 1999; quote from p. 6.)

7. Michael Ray and Rochelle Myers argue that everyone has an inner creative resource, which they call one's "essence." The essence has several qualities that enable creativity—intuition (a "direct knowing without conscious reasoning"), a will or desire to create, joy from experiencing the process of creativity, strength to break through fear of criticism, and compassion for oneself and

others. (M. Ray and R. Myers, *Creativity in Business,* New York: Doubleday, 1986; quote from p. 8.)

8. Michael Ray and Rochelle Myers argue that anxiety and fear inhibit creativity (ibid.).

9. Scholars who study the impact of demographic diversity have argued that heterogeneous groups can be more creative and innovative, leading to better problem solving and decision making. The different perceptions and perspectives that different people offer can be the source of new ideas and opportunities. (For a review of the diversity literature, see, K. Y. Williams and C. A. O'Reilly, "Demography and diversity in organizations: A review of 40 years of research," in *Research and Organizational Behavior,* vol. 20, 1998, pp. 77–140.)

However, simply bringing people who are different from one another to work together will not necessarily lead to these positive outcomes. To benefit from diversity, groups and organizations need to link it to their core work in a manner that makes diversity a resource for learning and change. They also need to take actions to listen to, and to change in response to, the diverse viewpoints that are expressed. (See, e.g., R. J. Ely and D. A. Thomas, "Cultural diversity at work: The effects of diversity perspectives on work group processes and outcomes," *Administrative Science Quarterly,* vol. 46, 2001, pp. 228–273; L. Bailyn, *Breaking the Mold,* New York: Free Press, 1993.)

10. For a review of research on organizational learning, see S. B. Sitkin, K. M. Sutcliffe, and K. E. Weick, "Organizational learning," in R. C. Dorf, ed., *The Technology Management Handbook,* Boca Raton, Fla.: CRC Press, 1999.

See also work by Chris Argyris, who distinguishes between single-loop and double-loop learning in organizations. In single-loop learning, organizations take corrective actions but still carry on with their present standards and objectives. Argyris compares this type of learning to a thermostat, which takes corrective action when it is too hot or cold by turning the heat on or off. In double-loop learning, organizations question their actual standards and objectives. They don't just take corrective actions to meet the standards and objectives in place, they explore and experiment with new standards and objectives. In other words, in double-loop learning, organizations question the actual temperature at which the thermostat is set. (C. Argyris and D. Schon, *Organizational Learning: A Theory of Action Perspective,* Reading, Mass.: Addison-Wesley, 1978; C. Argyris, *Overcoming Organizational Defenses: Facilitating Organizational Learning,* Upper Saddle River, N.J.: Prentice Hall, 1990.)

11. Learning in a group or organization takes place when there is both new knowledge or insight *and* new or modified behavior (D. Garvin, *Learning in Action,* Boston: Harvard Business School Press, 2000).

12. Amy Edmondson's research on team learning has found that when team members do not express different opinions and information, the team doesn't gain new knowledge and new ways of working (A. Edmondson, "The local and variegated nature of learning in organizations: A group level perspective," *Organization Science,* vol. 13, no. 2, 2002, pp. 128–146).

13. Organizational scholars have described how problems persist and are not corrected because people are not comfortable with speaking up about them openly—thus preventing organizational learning (see, e.g., Argyris and Schon, *Organizational Learning* [note 10 above]; C. Argyris, "Double loop learning in organizations," *Harvard Business Review,* vol. 55, no. 5, 1977, pp. 115–129; M. Beer and R. E. Eisenstadt, "The silent killers of strategy implementation and learning," *Sloan Management Review,* vol. 41, Summer 2000, pp. 29–40).

14. Louis Barnes specifically points out that not giving feedback to someone who needs it is one of the cruelest things one can do because it denies the other person information that could make a difference in their future performance (L. B. Barnes, "Managing interpersonal feedback," Harvard Business School Teaching Note, 1982).

15. The notion of the Abilene Paradox comes from Jerry Harvey, "The Abilene Paradox: The management of agreement," *Organizational Dynamics,* Summer 1974, pp. 63–80.

16. The quotes used in recounting the story and the excerpt in italics come directly from Harvey, ibid., pp. 63–65.

17. The idea of using the Watergate incident as an example of

the Abilene Paradox comes from Jerry Harvey (ibid., pp. 68–69), who draws on details of the incident from reports in the *Washington Post.*

18. *Washington Post,* June 8, 1973, p. 20 (as cited in Harvey, ibid., p. 68).

19. *Washington Post,* June 15, 1973, p. A14 (as cited in Harvey, ibid., p. 69).

20. Harvey in particular describes the problem of the Abilene Paradox as mismanagement of agreement—that is, people agree with one another, but they don't realize it because no one speaks up as to their true beliefs. Harvey specifically focuses on decisions in which there is underlying *agreement.* (Harvey, ibid., p. 66.)

21. Irving Janis's "groupthink" is also about how groups make bad decisions because doubts or concerns are not expressed regarding the group's unanimous choice (I. Janis, *Groupthink,* Boston: Houghton Mifflin, 1982).

Groupthink is similar to the Abilene Paradox, but there is no requirement in groupthink for underlying agreement. Janis focuses his analysis of group decision making on the faulty decision-making process (such as failing to look at all the information available) and explores the dynamics and norms that pressure people into going along with the group decision (such as "self-appointed mindguards," which are individual members who talk dissenters into agreeing with the group consensus). Jerry Harvey, in contrast, focuses his analysis of the Abilene Paradox more on individual members' decisions about whether to speak up as related to the perceived costs and benefits of differing from the group. I focus on the norms and pressures people experience as well as on individuals' assessment of the risks and benefits of speaking up, which helps them decide how to respond to those norms and pressures.

22. Charlan Nemeth's research focuses on the effect of dissenting voices or minority opinions on group decision making and problem solving. She has found that even just one dissenting voice—that is, one person expressing an opinion that differs from the majority opinion—can force other group members to reexamine their own positions and look at issues from a wider variety of perspectives (i.e., "divergent thinking"), thus enhancing group performance. (See, e.g., C. J. Nemeth, "Managing innovation: When

less is more," *California Management Review,* 1997, vol. 40, no. 1, pp. 59–74; ibid., "Dissent, group process and creativity," *Advances in Group Processes,* vol. 2, 1985, pp. 57–75.)

CHAPTER FIVE

1. Research has shown the pace of life to be accelerating in recent decades and possibly even since the Middle Ages (see, e.g., J. Gleick, *Faster: The Acceleration of Just About Everything,* New York: Vintage, 2000; J. P. Robinson and G. Godbey, *Time for Life: The Surprising Ways Americans Use Their Time,* University Park: University of Pennsylvania Press, 1997; J. Schor, *The Overworked American: The Unexpected Decline of Leisure,* New York: Basic Books, 1992).

2. Numerous people have touted the benefits of speed-based competitive strategies (see, e.g., C. Meyer, *Fast Cycle Time: How to Align Purpose, Strategy, and Structure for Speed,* New York: Free Press, 1993; G. Stalk and T. Hout, *Competing Against Time: How Time-Based Competition is Reshaping Global Markets,* New York: Free Press, 1990).

3. See, for example, Gleick, *Faster,* pp. 6–7 (note 1 above); J. Rifkin, *Time Wars: The Primary Conflict in Human History,* New York: Holt, 1987; Robinson and Godbey, *Time for Life,* pp. 29–30 (note 1 above).

4. P. LaBarre, "Keith Yamashita wants to reinvent your company," *Fast Company,* no. 64, November 2002, p. 88.

5. Gleick, *Faster* (note 1 above); quote from back cover.

6. For more information on how critical fast cycle time—including new product development—is to a company's competitive advantage and how companies can effectively reduce their cycle times, see, e.g., J. L. Bower and T. M. Hout, "Fast-cycle time capability for competitive power," *Harvard Business Review,* November–December 1988; Meyer, *Fast Cycle Time* (note 2 above).

7. Research suggests that more diversity of ideas and more deliberation over ideas can lead to better-quality decisions (see, e.g., K. A. Bantel and S. E. Jackson, "Top management and innovations in banking: Does the composition of the top team make a difference?" *Strategic Management Journal,* vol. 10, 1989, pp.

107–112; D. Hickson, R. Butler, D. Cray, G. Mallory, and D. Wilson, *Top Decisions: Strategic Decision Making in Organizations*, San Francisco: Jossey-Bass, 1986; H. Mintzberg, D. Raisinghani, and A. Theoret, "The structure of 'unstructured' decision processes," *Administrative Science Quarterly*, vol. 21, 1976, pp. 246–275).

However, since more deliberation can also slow down the decision-making process, people are more likely to bypass such elements of effective decision making when they are under pressure to work quickly (L. A. Perlow, G. A. Okhuysen, and N. P. Repenning, "The speed trap: Exploring the relationship between decision making and the temporal context," *Academy of Management Journal*, vol. 45, 2002, pp. 931–955).

8. Research on the effects of time pressure has shown that time pressure increases the rate of individual and group performance (see, e.g., J. R. Kelly, G. C. Futoran, and J. E. McGrath, "Capacity and capability: Seven studies of entrainment of task performance rates," *Small Group Research*, vol. 21, 1990, pp. 283–314; E. A. Locke and G. P. Latham, *A Theory of Goal Setting and Task Performance*, Englewood Cliffs, N.J.: Prentice Hall, 1990).

However, the effect of time pressure on quality of performance is less clear. As Janice Kelly and Steve Karau describe, some research has found a negative linear relationship between time pressure and performance quality, while other research has found a curvilinear relationship between time pressure and performance quality (suggesting that best-quality performance is achieved with a moderate amount of time pressure). According to Kelly and Karau, the difference in the shape of the time pressure-performance quality relationship (linear vs. curvilinear) depends on the kinds of tasks and the measures of quality. (J. R. Kelly and S. J. Karau, "Entrainment of creativity in small groups," *Small Group Research*, vol. 24, 1993, pp. 179–198.)

9. Deadlines or pressure to go fast—such as from the need to develop and introduce new products and services—can be a motivation to redesign work and work processes so that they are made more efficient (see, e.g., Meyer, *Fast Cycle Time*; note 2 above).

In collaboration with a team of software engineers at a high-tech Fortune 500 company, I used the goal of constraining their long work hours (a result of pressure to have a short product development cycle) as a catalyst to find new ways of working. It became apparent that the underlying reason the engineers had to work the long hours that they did was that only early in the morning. late at night, and on the weekends could they find time to focus on their individual technical problem solving. We therefore agreed to incorporate some of that precious quiet time into their normal workday. Three days a week, blocks of time were set aside when individuals could not interrupt each other. Through this experiment with "quiet time," engineers learned that if they interrupted each other less they could get more done in less time. And, as a result, they became more conscientious about how they used their time and about the effects they were having on others' time. Moreover, after experimenting with quiet time, their product launched on time, one of the first on-time launches in this division's history. (L. Perlow, *Finding Time: How Corporations, Individuals, and Families Can Benefit from New Work Practices*, Ithaca, N.Y.: Cornell University Press, 1997.)

10. For example, Christopher Meyer explains that redesigning work processes is a critical component in effectively reducing cycle time because it enables people to focus on value-added tasks and eliminate nonessential ones (Meyer, *Fast Cycle Time*; note 2 above).

11. George Stalk and Thomas Hout argue that successful companies today offer a greater variety of products and services in much less time than their competitors. Successful companies have also been able to provide their products and services at lower cost because their own costs have declined, in part, because of greater worker and manufacturing efficiency. (Stalk and Hout, *Competing Against Time*; note 2 above.)

12. For example, Peter Senge notes that if not done correctly, trying to "speed up" cycle times in companies can result in workers becoming more over-stretched and managers becoming even more focused on crises (Peter Senge, "Foreword," in Meyer, *Fast Cycle Time*; note 2 above).

13. For more detailed substantiation of each of the links that explain how silencing conflict is both perpetuated by, and perpetu-

ates, the sense of urgency, as well as additional feedback processes at play, see Perlow, Okhuysen, and Repenning, "The speed trap" (note 7 above). In this paper, my colleagues Gerardo Okhuysen and Nelson Repenning and I distill the data from the ethnographic study of Versity using causal loop diagrams. We show how a need for fast action became a product of Versity's own past emphasis on speed. We focus more generally on the decision-making process, but one core element of the decision-making process is how differences are handled. And the more one silences differences, the more quickly decisions can be made. When one favors the speed of decision making over the content, though, it turns out that the decisions are increasingly likely to generate future problems, creating a vicious cycle of rising urgency, declining attention to content, and mounting problems.

CHAPTER SIX

1. Most of the scenes depicted in this part of the book took place while I was physically present. However, there are some scenes in which I've pieced together characters' thoughts or actions on the basis of extensive interviews.

2. Kevin O'Connor was the only participant interviewed for this study whose real name appears in the book. His role as CEO of DoubleClick is of particular importance to the story and it would be impossible to identify him as DoubleClick's CEO and yet successfully hide his true identity.

3. As described in Chapter 4, teams whose members express differences have the potential to produce more creative results and make better decisions. When team members feel comfortable expressing their differences, the team will have more information and perspectives from which to view the task or problem. Further, they will be more likely to think of their task or problem in new and different ways and, as a result, more likely to explore new and different solutions. For people's differences to have this positive effect, however, the team must value these differences and link them to their core work in a way that enables them to use their differences as a resource for learning and change.

CHAPTER SEVEN

1. E-mail communications tend to be more impulsive and blunt because there are less tangible reminders of the other person. When messages are communicated through e-mail, people often convey stronger emotions than they might do otherwise—which may be good or bad depending on the situation. (L. Sproull and S. Kiesler, *Connections: New Ways of Working in the Networked Organization,* Cambridge: MIT Press, 1991.)

Moreover, when someone communicates via e-mail, the other person receives the message void of nonverbal cues and other aspects of the context. Therefore, while initiating a conversation about differences through e-mail may sometimes be effective, it is probably better to follow up and continue the conversation face-to-face so that each person has the maximum opportunity to understand the other.

2. Peter's behavior reflects a common tendency among managers. According to Robert Blake and Jane Mouton, when asked to address something that might hurt their employees' feelings or cause discomfort, managers often choose to say nothing (R. Blake and J. Mouton, *The Managerial Grid III,* Houston: Gulf Publishing, 1985).

3. See Edgar Schein for a discussion of the role leaders play in creating and perpetuating cultural assumptions (E. H. Schein, *Organizational Culture and Leadership,* San Francisco: Jossey-Bass, 1991).

CHAPTER NINE

1. The Nasdaq peaked on March 10, 2000, at 5,048.62 and then dropped 1,727.33, or 34.2 percent, during the five weeks that followed (quotes of the Nasdaq composite index from Yahoo! Finance). Dot-com companies started going out of business on a regular basis, and it was very difficult for any company, especially Internet companies, to go public at this time (J. Cassidy, *Dot.con: The Greatest Story Ever Sold,* New York: HarperCollins, 2002).

2. J. C. Collins and J. I. Porras, *Built to Last,* New York: HarperBusiness, 1997.

3. E. D. Shaw, "The insider problem," *Information Security Magazine,* January 2001.

4. Not only has IZIO survived but so have both of its major competitors—Blackboard and WebCT. Blackboard offers online education products and services (such as course management tools and distance learning) to universities, primary and secondary school systems, and even corporations. They now have a long list of clients from around the world and as of the third quarter, 2002, have achieved profitability. WebCT also provides very similar online education products and services to higher education institutions in more than 80 countries.

CHAPTER TEN

1. As I described in Chapter 4, the cost of silence is that we lose out in terms of creativity, learning, and the health of our relationships. The flip side is that when we express differences effectively, we facilitate creativity and learning. Effectively expressing difference has also been shown to benefit relationships. For example, Jean Baker Miller and Irene Stiver have described relationships in which the partners are open and honest and as a result feel a sense of connection. Connection is something that people can experience within their relationships only when they are acting authentically and listening to and understanding the other person's authentic self. Connection is also mutually empowering in that people feel a sense of "zest" or energy from it and desire to have more connection. Miller and Stiver further suggest that connection provides a continuing source of growth and fosters psychological health. (J. B. Miller and I. P. Stiver, *The Healing Connection,* Boston: Beacon Press, 1997.)

2. Often people do not consider speaking up about differences to be their responsibility. They blame others for causing the conflict and therefore wait for them to address it first. (See, e.g., J. Kottler, *Beyond Blame: A New Way of Resolving Conflicts in Relationships,* San Francisco: Jossey-Bass, 1994.)

Frequently, people also do not consider speaking up to be part of their job, or what is required or expected of them in their given position or job. Linn Van Dyne and Jeffrey LePine have found that many people consider "voice" (or speaking up to suggest changes even when others disagree) as an extra-role behavior—that is, a behavior that goes above and beyond what is required or expected of them. (L. Van Dyne and J. A. LePine, "Helping and voice extra-role behaviors: Evidence of construct and predictive validity," *Academy of Management Journal*, vol. 41, 1998, pp. 108–119.)

3. Harriet Lerner, *The Dance of Anger*, New York: Harper & Row, 1985, p. 14.

4. The notion of "talking tough" comes from Otto Scharmer's work. People engage in "talking tough" when they speak their mind and advocate their own position. Talking tough, however, doesn't involve seeking to understand the other person's views. (C. O. Scharmer, "Self-transcending knowledge: Organizing around emerging realities," in I. Nonaka and D. Teece, eds., *Managing Industrial Knowledge: Creation, Transfer and Utilization*, Thousand Oaks, Calif.: Sage, 2001, pp. 68–90.)

5. This definition of open-ended questions—as questions that give the other person broad latitude in how to answer—comes from D. Stone, B. Patton, and S. Heen, *Difficult Conversations*, New York: Penguin, 1999, p. 174.

6. Michael Beer points out that one of the roles a manager can take in a performance review meeting is that of a helper. This helps to eliminate defensiveness and better encourages change. (M. Beer, "Conducting a performance appraisal interview," Harvard Business School Teaching Note, 1997.)

7. Chris Argyris writes about the need to shift from a "Model I" to a "Model II" way of operating. Model I is Argyris's term for the way of operating in which people react to things that embarrass or threaten them by covering up the issue. Model II, in contrast, is Argyris's term for a desirable state in which misunderstandings, errors, self-fulfilling prophecies, and self-sealing processes are reduced. To operate in Model II requires being forthright and providing data so the other person can see how one arrived at one's conclusion and so the conclusion itself can be examined further. Model II requires continually questioning any conclusions or interpretations so that people are not making biased judgments without evaluating all the information. Model II does not require a softer and more forgiving approach to manage-

ment. Rather, it demands a more proactive approach to problems. (C. Argyris, *Overcoming Organizational Defenses,* Upper Saddle River, N.J.: Prentice Hall, 1990.)

8. Peter Senge promotes the practice of balancing advocacy and inquiry to facilitate learning in organizations. Advocacy involves stating one's views; inquiry involves asking questions to understand another's views. When people practice advocacy and inquiry together, they shift the goal of solving problems and making decisions from trying to win an argument to working with others to find the best argument. Senge argues that most managers are trained to be advocates. And for them to incorporate inquiry into how they interact, they need not only to inquire into what's behind another person's views but also to learn to state their own views in a way that invites others to ask questions about those views. (P. Senge, *The Fifth Discipline: The Art and Practice of the Learning Organization,* New York: Doubleday, 1990, pp. 198–202.)

9. The Herman Miller example comes from William Isaacs (W. Isaacs, "The perils of shared ideals," in P. Senge, A. Kleiner, C. Roberts, R. Ross, G. Roth, and B. Smith, eds., *The Dance of Change: The Challenges to Sustaining Momentum in Learning Organizations,* New York: Doubleday, 1999, pp. 350–352).

10. Deborah Kolb and Judith Williams describe the notion of a "turn" in a negotiation. According to Kolb and Williams, turns help to "resist attempts to put you in your place" by reframing the situation. Kolb and Williams describe a number of ways that one can make a turn: interrupt the action (for example, by calling for a time-out, so that one can think about how to deal with the situation), name the other person's "move" or action they have taken to further the negotiation (i.e., let the other party know outright that one is aware of what is going on), correct the move (i.e., offer an alternative explanation for an issue in the negotiation that puts one in a more positive light), and divert the move (i.e., shift the discussion away from the personal to the problem). (D. Kolb and J. Williams, *The Shadow Negotiation,* New York: Simon & Schuster, 2000; quotes from p. 106.)

11. On the basis of extensive lab studies, Serge Moscovici has shown that when a minority is brave enough to reject established order or to propose something previously thought "forbidden,"

their actions prove that there are other acceptable ways and that acting and living in these alternative ways do not necessarily have the direct consequences feared. When it is proven that refusal is possible, norms are stripped of their authority. (S. Moscovici, *Social Influence and Social Change*, London: Academic Press, 1976.)

12. Serge Moscovici further shows how deviance forces the majority to suddenly confront the possibility that alternatives exist. Deviance casts doubt on the infallibility of the majority's judgment by entertaining a different possibility of achieving the same end goal and explaining the same phenomenon. Deviance is a threat to the assumed consensus as it proposes a new alternative. (Moscovici, ibid.)

13. According to Karl Weick, a small win is a "concrete, complete, implemented outcome of moderate importance" (K. E. Weick, "Small wins: Redefining the scale of social problems," *American Psychologist*, vol. 39, 1984, p. 43).

In her book *Tempered Radicals*, Debra Meyerson further suggests that because small wins are doable, they create a sense of hope, self-efficacy, and confidence. Meyerson describes how leveraging small wins is an effective strategy for making significant change in organizations. (D. Meyerson, *Tempered Radicals*, Boston: Harvard Business School Press, 2001.)

14. This fairy tale is drawn from Hans Christian Andersen, *The Complete Fairy Tales and Stories*, trans. by E. C. Haugaard, New York: Anchor Books, 1983, pp. 77–81.

15. For a discussion of the functionality of deviance, see J. Van Maanen, "The self, situation, and the rules of interpersonal relations," in W. Bennis, J. Van Maanen, E. Schein, and F. Steele, eds., *Essays in Interpersonal Dynamics*, Homewood, Ill.: Dorsey Press, 1979, pp. 43–101.

16. As Chris Argyris points out, one would not want to express every sentiment felt during a business meeting, but by learning to examine critically one's feelings and concerns, one can better identify the key issues and communicate them without the ambiguity that often creates misunderstanding and eventually resentment (Argyris, *Overcoming Organizational Defenses;* note 7 above).

CHAPTER ELEVEN

1. The account here is primarily taken from a published talk in which Nancy Hopkins tells her story (N. Hopkins, "Experience of women at the Massachusetts Institute of Technology," in *Women in the Chemical Workforce: A Workshop Report to the Chemical Sciences Roundtable,* Commission on Physical Sciences, Mathematics, and Applications, National Academy Press, 2000, pp. 110–124).

My understanding of Hopkins's efforts was further enhanced by descriptions in a number of other places, including Lotte Bailyn, "Academic careers and gender equity: Lessons learned from MIT," in *Gender, Work and Organizations,* March 2003; Ellen Goodman, "Feminism hits home for the women on MIT's faculty," *Boston Globe,* April 11, 1999, p. D7; Debra Meyerson, *Tempered Radicals,* Boston: HBS Press, 2001; Robin Wilson, "An MIT professor's suspicion of bias leads to a new movement for academic women," *Chronicle of Higher Education,* Dec. 3, 1999.

2. Hopkins, "Experience of women," p. 111 (note 1 above).

3. Ibid.

4. Ibid, p. 112.

5. Ibid.

6. Ibid.

7. Ibid., pp. 112–113.

8. Ibid., p. 113.

9. Bailyn, "Academic careers," p. 20 (note 1 above). This is a direct quote from Bailyn's article, in which she paraphrases the dean in these words. To avoid suggesting that these words come directly from the dean, however, quotation marks have been omitted in the text.

10. The same principle—that a group of people together can have a bigger impact on creating change than an individual—holds true at many different levels, from small collectives in organizations to national civil rights movements (M. Zald and M. Berger, "Social movements in organizations: Coup d'état, insurgency and mass movements," *American Journal of Sociology,* vol. 83, 1978, pp. 823–861).

11. The phrase "an air of confident knowledge" comes from

P. Senge, *The Fifth Discipline,* New York: Currency/Doubleday, 1990, p. 251.

12. Clearly ensuring that people's raises and promotions are not negatively affected by their openness can be aided by larger structural changes, such as making alterations to the formal reward system itself. If you have the authority to make structural changes, they are a valuable lever for creating the conditions that enable people to speak up. Ultimately, effective organizations require a high degree of fit between the informal and formal organization. (D. A. Nadler and M. L. Tushman, *Competing by Design,* New York: Oxford University Press, 1997.)

ACKNOWLEDGMENTS

This book was a long time in the making and I received incredible support and guidance along the way. I will never be able to do justice to the type of dedication and commitment this book drew from people. All I can do here is to thank them, and hope that they know how invaluable they were in the process. First and foremost, I am deeply grateful to the many students, friends, family members, colleagues, casual acquaintances, and complete strangers who were willing to share their experiences and perspectives with me. The people of Versity.com deserve special mention; they let me share in their company's roller-coaster ride from dorm room to incredible heights in the Silicon Valley to bankruptcy.

Beyond the people who provided the data for this book are those who helped to research and write it. My first stroke of good luck was finding Margaret DiLaura, a former student of mine at the University of Michigan. In order to help me study life at Versity, she opted to postpone her senior year in college and follow the founders to Silicon Valley. After the company went bankrupt, and I got to work writing their story, I had the good fortune to cross paths with Nikki Sabin. A former editor of HBS Press, she spent an entire summer helping me think through the dot-com story. It was my editor at Crown Business, John Mahaney, who encouraged me to take the book to the next level and conduct interviews far beyond the dot-com world. And it was as I embarked on this further exploration that I had the wonderful fortune of calling an old friend and favorite colleague from Michigan, Stephanie Williams, to find that she had just left her own dot-com experience and was looking for work. For the next year she worked as my far overqualified research associate—with a Ph.D. herself—helping me conduct interviews, analyze data, and read all the relevant literature.

And, as if those people were not enough good fortune, throughout the process I found myself continually surrounded by deeply supportive, giving, and insightful colleagues, friends, and family members. The following people all read part of the manuscript, many of them a complete draft, and some many more than just one draft: Lotte Bailyn, Max Bazerman, Michael Beer, Jennifer Chatman, Joshua Coval, Jane Dutton, Martha Feldman, Jack Gabarro, Mauro Guillen, Connie Hale, Linda Hill, Deborah Kolb, Jay and Linda Land, Paul Lawrence, Mie-Yun Lee, Jay Lorsch, John Mahaney, Heather McPhee, Jill MacQuarrie, Jon Perlow, Joy Perlow, Kim Perlow, Thomas Popik, Robert Quinn, Nelson Repenning, Edgar Schein, Scott Snook, Mary Anne Stewart, David Thomas, John Van Maanen, John Weeks, Will Weiser, Richard Williams, Howard Yoon, and Denise Zarn. Nitin Nohria didn't just read more drafts of the manuscript than I would like to admit existed, but he guided me through the endless aspects of writing a book.

Others who helped me in the process include my assistant Joan McDonald, my agent Gail Ross, and my longtime friend and colleague Joshua Margolis (who taught six classes on one day so I could attend the Versity vision meeting).

I am grateful not only to all the people who helped me but to the organizations that provided me financial support. Both the Sloan Foundation and the Harvard Business School division of research were extremely generous in enabling me to conduct this study and write it up.

And finally, I cannot say enough thanks to my family, who put up with me for all these years as I stayed buried away writing and rewriting and promising that I really was almost done this time. They were there for support and they were there to endlessly test out my ideas. I could always trust that they would speak up and express their views. Thank you Mom, Dad, Kim, and Josh.

INDEX